# DANCING TO THE
# RHYTHM OF MY SOUL

# DANCING TO THE RHYTHM OF MY SOUL

*A Sister's Guide for Transforming Madness into Gladness*

RHONDA R. SWAN

Also by Rhonda Swan

*Busted: Never Underestimate a Sista's Revenge*

*Speaking My Mind...in Poetic Verse*

Published by Conscious Mind Press

Library of Congress Control Number:
2011903421
Printed in the United States of America
Published by Conscious Mind Press
First Edition

10 9 8 7 6 5 4 3 2 1

*In memory of my grandmothers, Sallie Mary Johnson Swan and Alice Fason Brown and in honor of my aunt, Dorothy Swan Scott, women of faith who walked the talk and led by example.*

# ACKNOWLEDGMENTS

I am grateful to my spiritual partner Benn Johnson for guiding and encouraging me along my journey. To my aunt, Agnes Johnson, for introducing me to a great spiritual teacher. To my mother, DeLois Swan, for her unconditional love, her courage and her strength. To my dad, Fred Swan, Sr. for encouraging me to seek my own truths. And to the strong women in my corner; my sister Freda Malone and my sister-friends, Zahira Vargas and Arlene Smith.

I'm also grateful to David Rosa, my significant other, who has been the catalyst for so much of my spiritual growth, and who unwittingly prompted me to write this book.

Also, to my editor Susan Barnett for polishing my prose and making it shine.

# CONTENTS

# INTRODUCTION

Are you living your best life? Are you happy with the way things are right now in this moment? Or are you wounded, stuck in the past and filled with regrets? Perhaps you're stalled in neutral, waiting for something that you believe will make you complete.

So often we find ourselves at a rest stop on life's highway, unhappy with the way things are but too afraid, lazy or tired to change them. We settle for partners that don't treat us the way we deserve because we fear the next one won't be any better or, worse, there won't *be* a next one. We settle for jobs that we hate for pretty much the same reason. We stay in cities that limit our growth because the thought of leaving overwhelms us. We attend religious services out of habit and obligation even when they fail to provide nourishment for our souls. Why? Because believing something different, doing something different, being someone different means change.

For many of us, change is a scary proposition. It means venturing into the unknown. Often, though, the unknown is what gets us to happy.

My hope is that this book will help you see how changing your thoughts, changing your perceptions, changing how you respond to the people and events in your life can bring you joy and inner peace. I hope it also will give you the strength and courage to make the changes that may be exactly what you need to grow. Too many of us stay wounded even though healing is right within our reach.

There was a time not long ago when I was drowning in the quicksand of my past, unable to break free of the vice grip of regrets. I was MAD – Miserable, Angry and Defensive. I blamed everything and everyone for my lot in life. It took me years, though, to recognize that I was angry. And to realize that my anger was the external manifestation of internal pain.

At one point, I was so depressed that I lost 20 pounds. I tried to force myself to eat, but nothing stayed down and I had no idea why.

I know now that it's because I had become a human garbage disposal and the tank was full. Filled with toxic emotions that I had unconsciously suppressed.

When you know better, you do better. Today, I am GLAD - Grateful, Loving, Aware and Divine. I know that connecting with my soul is the source of my power. I call that feeling of connectedness dancing to the rhythm of my soul. It's a lot healthier than dancing to the beat of my ego.

I hope that by sharing my story - and snippets of the stories of others - my sisters in the spirit also will strive to dance to the rhythm of their souls.

I believe that my dharma – my life's purpose – is to use my writing to encourage and enlighten. To share my knowledge so that it might help someone else. Life is amazing when we let go of hurt, anger, and resentment and open ourselves up to the miracles that enlightenment and change can bring.

Namaste,
Rhonda

# Confessions of an Angry Black Woman

*~ Holding on to anger is like grasping a hot coal with the intent of throwing it at someone else; you are the one who gets burned. ~ Buddha*

My name is Rhonda and I'm a recovering Angry Black Woman. I used to take pleasure in knowing that people found me intimidating. I wore the title Bitch with pride. Bragged that I had zero tolerance for bullshit. Rarely let down my guard. Was hyper critical and judgmental. Blamed the outside world for everything that went wrong inside my world.

My father wasn't there for me when I was growing up. The fathers of my children were triflin' and left me to raise them on my own.

So what! I was a strong black woman. I didn't need a man. I could make it by myself. Earned a degree. Got a good job and bought a house without the help of a man. Still, I constantly had to prove myself. Prove that I was just as smart, just as good, just as qualified as my white colleagues. Specifically, the male ones.

Most of my co-workers kept their distance. I didn't stepin fetchit enough for them and that must have appeared to be a threat. All black women carry knives, you know.

It gets tiresome carrying the burden of the black female stereotype with you to work every day. Plus I was carrying the torch for the entire black community in the newsroom where I worked. But did my community appreciate the stress and the bullshit I went through? Hell, no! To them, I was another member of the establishment that was always trying to make black people look bad.

And I got angry. Public beware. I'm dragging a lot of dead weight around so don't get in my way. Servers, don't even think about getting my order wrong. Not only will I send it back, I'll rip you a new one for making the mistake. Brothers, don't expect me to smile when you approach to make your move. Been down that road. Got the T-shirt and the fatherless children – one, who's been shot, and another who's served nearly six years behind bars - to prove it. Slow drivers, speed up or get the hell out of my way. Grocers, if I have to stand in line all day to give you my money it's going to get ugly!

Ditto for doctors, dentists and anyone else that tries my patience. I have no problem speaking my mind and my words will leave a mark!

Whew! Sound like someone you know? It's OK to admit if that someone is you. The first step to recovery is admitting you have a problem. The truth is a lot of us wake up angry, walk around angry and go to bed angry. And even if we don't want to admit it, anger is a helluva problem.

I was a bona fide member of the sisterhood of Angry Black Women. But I was in denial. I wasn't the media stereotype of the Angry Black Woman, the one who doesn't speak, but shrieks. She blames. She shames. She snaps. And she saps all the energy out of the room.

She is the head shaking, hip grabbing, eye-rolling sista with a boulder on her shoulder we see on TV and in movies. She didn't look like me or any of the sisters in my circle. She was, in my mind, a figment of Hollywood's imagination and of black men's exaggeration.

Then one day, I caught a glimpse of her and realized she did, in fact, exist. I was looking in the mirror and the Angry Black Woman staring back was me!

Most angry people don't know they're angry. We don't see ourselves in Tasha Mack, the character that Wendy Raquel Robinson portrays so fabulously on the TV show, *The Game,* or in any of the other loud and angry black females we see in the media; women like Nene Leakes and Sheree Whitfield of *The Real Housewives of Atlanta* or Evelyn Lozado and Tami Roman of *Basketball Wives*. We laugh at the screaming, cat fighting housewives on reality TV. Because we're not loud, crass or ignorant, we think we're not one of them.

Wrong! Don't get stuck on the word *angry* or the stereotypical dramatic behavior we associate with anger. Anger often wears a mask, hiding behind a disguise of strength, pride, self-respect, and confidence. So when other people look at us and see anger, defensiveness, hostility, arrogance and invulnerability, we wonder where in the world they came up with that assessment. We see ourselves as independent, strong, responsible, and self-assured.

*You will not be punished for your anger; you will be punished by your anger. ~ Buddha*

Whatever attributes our ego needs for its survival will stick to us like Velcro. And we'll be proud, not realizing that what we're doing is building walls that keep us miserable.

We will hold on to this anger until something makes us realize that while it may be essential for the survival of our ego, it will be the spiritual death of our soul. And that soul is the essence of who we truly are. To connect with our soul, the anger must go.

The ego is our representative. It is the "I am" that we present to the world as defined by our experiences and beliefs. It is the essence of our personality and makes us the unique individuals that we are. The ego controls how we react to and perceive the outside world. Those reactions and perceptions, however, are usually based on fear. Fear of rejection, fear of loneliness, fear of being perceived as less than.

If we dared to look inside, we'd find we're vulnerable, sensitive, and longing to be loved.

Each of us has a story. Our personal history of tragedies and triumphs, successes and disappointments help define our personalities. However, as a group, black women in the U.S. share a common history, and as a result, a common present.

You know the statistics. Far more black women are attending college than black men. We also are getting better quality jobs and making more money. This has created an uneven field on which to play the mating game.

Too many of our men define themselves by how many women they can bed and how much money they can make by any means necessary.

Too many of us grow up without fathers or positive male role models. In turn, we choose boys that look like men as mates nd end up raising our children alone.

And we're angry about it.

Despite the strides we've made in corporate America, we still have to work twice as hard to get equal recognition.

Government studies show that black women work harder and earn less. In 2012, the Bureau of Labor Statistics found that black women earned on average only 70 percent for every dollar white men earn each week; 88 percent of what white women earn; and 93 percent of what black men earn.

We're still playing catch up. And we're angry about it.

We're upset that most of the time we see ourselves on TV or in the movies, we're hookers, drug addicts, lazy, uneducated, baby mamas, gold diggers, and video hoes. Our men are depicted as gang bangers, thugs, drug dealers, and rappers.

Many of us are alone. Not by choice, but because we bought into the common refrain that the pickings are slim. Black men with a good heart and a good job exist but not, it seems, in the places we look. When we do see them, they are gay, shacking, married or prefer women who don't look like us. So if we're not ready to cross that color line, we spend our Saturday nights alone.

And we are damn angry about it!

# Dancing to the Rhythm of My Soul

Even with Barack and Michelle Obama in the White House, being black in America is still a hard road to hoe and black women have still got far to go.

Black women are not the only women who are angry. But we are the ones who get a bad rap for it. And certainly not all black women are angry. But many of us are. As a result, Angry Black Woman has become the new Bitch. We've taken the sting out of the B-word by using it as a term of endearment, so Angry Black Woman has become the way people denigrate and stereotype sisters. Angry is the new racial epithet for black women.

During the 2008 presidential campaign, Fox News' Bill O'Reilly said about Michelle Obama, "Now I have a lot of people who call me on the radio and say she looks angry. And I have to say there's some validity to that. She looks like an angry woman."

During the segment, O'Reilly asked Human Events columnist Michelle Oddis: "Is there any validity to that? Or is that an urban myth?" Oddis responded: "I wouldn't say it's an urban myth. I think we all can tell just by appearances and speeches and the way that Michelle has personified herself that she's not warm and fuzzy. We know that about her."

And that, ladies, was expected to be the nail in Michelle Obama's coffin. Call a black woman angry and everyone suddenly becomes scared of her. She walks into the room and people are supposed to scatter like roaches when the light comes on.

The right wing has even labeled Oprah Winfrey, one of the most generous, open, kindhearted and spiritually aware sisters on the planet, angry.

Unfortunately, this ubiquitous stereotype gives many of us who actually are angry an easy out. We can stay in denial by saying we've been pigeonholed by the media into this bogus role, and there's really nothing wrong with us.

For example, when the editor of the newspaper where I worked lashed out with a bad review on Amazon.com of my poetry book, *Speaking My Mind in Poetic Verse,* he wrote, "her amateurish attempts to posture herself as an angry black woman ring shallow and false."

He was peeved about a piece I titled, *The Newsroom,* in which I described my feelings about being the only black editor in our all-white news meetings. He didn't take kindly to my calling him the "head Caucasian in charge."

I wasn't, though, trying to posture myself as an angry black woman. I *was* an angry black woman. I just didn't realize it.

In hindsight, I realize that my former boss believed I was posturing because so many angry black women wear their anger as a badge of honor. The truth, however, is that anger is nothing more than a defense mechanism, a force field that keeps people from getting too close. If no one can get close, no one can hurt us.

Throughout my life, people have often stuck unflattering labels on me. Control freak, domineering, bossy, and macho are just a few.

Unfortunately, the people accusing me of these characteristics had their own character defects – men who were liars, cheaters, and often insecure – so they had no credibility. That made it easy to dismiss their characterization of me as false. But can everybody else be wrong, leaving me standing as the only one who is right?

What I've come to learn is that anger – or what others perceive as anger - often is the conscious manifestation of unconscious pain. Feelings that we bury do not disappear. Rejection, abandonment, disappointment, and loneliness don't just vanish. They pop up later disguised as something else. Pain that we never confront externalizes in a myriad of ways, including the need to always be in control. So-called control freaks are people who are afraid to be or appear powerless. That feeling of powerlessness exposes our vulnerabilities. And that is the last thing anyone, particularly a supposedly strong black woman, wants!

Angry people are actually wounded people. That's something Ms. Lozado and Ms. Roman are learning as they work on their emotional healing.

Most of us who are angry don't realize we are wounded because we've buried the pain so deep in an effort not to feel it. The truth is, eventually we will feel it. When anger arises it is seldom for the reason we think. More often, it's because something happening in the present has triggered an unresolved hurt from our past.

Often, we don't believe our anger is our problem because we can justify it by blaming it on someone else. For instance, I wouldn't have smashed that window out of my cheating ex-husband's car if he had just paid his child support! I had a right to be angry.

Even when our anger is justified, though, holding on to it only hurts us, not the person on whom we cast the blame. So it is *our* problem. Smashing that window didn't get me any child support. It didn't even make the anger disappear.

If you were being completely honest with yourself, how would you describe your emotional well-being? Go deep inside. What do you feel? Joy? Peace? Acceptance? Or is there pain? Turmoil? Resistance and regret?

Does any part of the description of Rhonda, the recovering Angry Black Woman, fit you?

If the answer is yes, realize that your emotional state is not permanent and you do have a choice in how you feel. Even if the reasons for your anger never disappear, your anger can. No matter how justified we believe our anger to be, we are angry because we choose to be angry. And we can choose not to be.

Nothing affects us but us. If we are going to stop being MAD – Miserable, Angry and Defensive – then we have to recognize that it's up to us to overcome these emotions and become GLAD – Grateful, Loving, Aware and Divine.

But we have to make a conscious decision to do that for ourselves. Nothing outside of us will help. Are you ready to choose gladness over madness?

## INNER WORK

### *OVERCOMING ANGER*

Write down all the people, places and events that make you angry or upset from small pet peeves to those that boil your blood. One at a time, analyze why each makes you feel the way they do. What unresolved issues from your past are they triggering?

Allow yourself to feel the pain and any other negative emotions that come up for each of these items.

Don't be afraid. Just sit with the feelings and let them have their way. Realize that the damage you've been inflicting on yourself by unconsciously denying the existence of these feelings is far worse than confronting them.

To let go of something, you first have to realize that *you* own it.

Breathe in deeply and then exhale.

Congratulate yourself for taking the first step to recovery. Do this exercise as often as is necessary for you to let go of that which makes anger arise within you.

# Attitude of Gratitude

---●●⬤●●---

*~ You simply will not be the same person two months from now after consciously giving thanks each day for the abundance that exists in your life. And you will have set in motion an ancient spiritual law: the more you have and are grateful for, the more will be given you. ~ Sarah Ban Breathnach - Simple Abundance: A Daybook of Comfort and Joy*

---●●⬤●●---

When the praises go up, the blessings come down. I spent many years attending a Pentecostal church where I often heard that saying. Too often, though, I found the congregants spent more time seeking blessings than they did sending up praises. Every Sunday, the same people would come to the altar to get prayer for a variety of ailments, trials and tribulations.

Rarely did I hear any of these individuals testify about any blessings that resulted from the prayers. I guess they were a secret!

One service that particularly stands out took place on New Year's Eve. It was our annual watch night service where we worshipped with members of another church to pray in the New Year. It's a tradition practiced by many Christian denominations.

I was home visiting for the holidays, but hadn't planned to attend the service because it usually put me to sleep. Ours wasn't exactly a jammin' church and neither was the Baptist congregation with whom we shared the service. Still, I let my sister talk me into going. We arrived in time for devotional service to find the devotion leaders begging people to testify and filling in the silence with a capella hymns sung off-key. Not exactly how I wanted to spend my New Year's.

The saints – that's what Pentecostals call church members who have accepted Jesus as their personal savior - sat motionless in their pews, coats on, no doubt watching the clock and praying for midnight. It was a scene I'd witnessed every New Year's Eve I could remember and during hundreds of other church services as well. I often wondered how church folk expected to draw new members – converts – when they were some of the most depressed, whiny people I'd ever seen in my life. Too often, when they did bother to testify it wasn't to give praise, but to vent about all they'd gone through during the week and how they had to press their way to church. Who would want to join a church to hear that on a regular basis? If God is so good and saints get so much joy every time they think about what He's done

14

for them - at least that's what they sing in their songs – then why did I so rarely see any joy?

*When we practice an attitude of gratitude, there's no room for anger. When we are busy being thankful for our abundance, we don't have time to find things about which to complain.*

This particular New Year's Eve I decided to speak my mind and say exactly that. After I expressed my gratitude at being home with my family – for which I was sincerely grateful – and for making it there safely over the highway from Virginia and my many other blessings, I told the congregation that I wanted to hear what they were grateful for. I reminded them that if nothing else, they had lived to see another year and that alone was something for which to be thankful.

The next thing I knew people were jumping out of their seats like popcorn waiting to give their testimony and send up the praises.

It's a wonderful feeling to think and talk about the good things that happen in our lives. Yet we seldom actually take the time to do so. We let negativity overwhelm us to a point where we act as though there is nothing in our lives for which to be grateful. But nothing could be further from the truth.

One of the first lessons I learned on my journey toward gladness was that I needed to be grateful. Many of us spend so much time focused on what we don't have – a good man, a nice house, a job we enjoy – that we forget about all the wonderful things we do have.

The negative energy we expend bemoaning the things we lack attracts more negative energy and ensures that we will continue to go without those very things. The moment we shift our focus to our blessings, we invite positive energy that enables those blessings to increase.

Thinking positively causes us to speak and act positively. When we do this, we draw positive people, things and situations into our lives. The opposite also is true. When we think negatively, we attract negative people, things and events.

So often people say they will expect the worse and hope for the best. This is a defense mechanism. We falsely believe that as long as we mentally prepare ourselves for the worst outcome, we won't be disappointed if it happens. We will have lost nothing because we have risked nothing. And if the best just so happens to occur, then we will, of course, be thrilled. And we use that as an excuse to continually expect the worse.

Doesn't it make more sense to expect the best?

# Dancing to the Rhythm of My Soul

I used to be the Queen of Negative Thoughts. I could always find something to complain about. The weather. My job. My relationship with a romantic partner or lack thereof. My finances. The result of this complaining was always the same. What was bad in my life became worse. And when it did, I could point to it as evidence that nothing ever went right for me. Plus, it gave me something else to complain about!

When I moved to South Florida, I quickly learned why my cousin, who had lived there only a few weeks, said it wasn't the place to be for a single black woman wanting a steady, monogamous relationship.

I went on several dates, but few led to a second. There was the man who worked at my credit union who invited me to dinner and waited until dessert to mention that, by the way, he was married! The Jamaican gentleman who needed a green card. A Haitian man who needed the same. Then there was the lawyer I went out with several times before he told me that he was separated from his wife and living with his girlfriend and her children. Still, he'd decided that I was his soul mate and he was willing to work out a deal – meaning pay a bill or two - if I would be in a monogamous relationship with him while he continued to juggle the other relationships in his life!

My boss joked that the dating pool in Palm Beach County was shallow. I said it was more like a puddle! And I said it over and over and over again. By the time I told the story of all these bad dates for the 100th time I realized that, perhaps, if I stopped telling it, my dates might get better!

I realized that I had been speaking into existence the very situation about which I was constantly complaining. I decided to develop an attitude of gratitude. Instead of focusing on what I didn't have, the right companion, I would focus on what I did have. My health. A great family that I could always count on. A job that paid my bills. A nice house in a decent neighborhood. And healthy children.

Things weren't so bad after all. In fact, simply waking up is a miracle for which to be grateful.

When I thought about all that I had to be thankful for, an internal shift took place. I became a much happier person. I decided that instead of focusing on what I wanted that I didn't have, I would claim it, be grateful and behave as though I did have it.

For example, though I was grateful for having a job because it provided the means by which I took care of myself and my children, I didn't like my job. I'd spent nine years as an editor. The hours were long and dealing with all the different personalities was too much like being a parent. That job is hard enough at home. I wanted to exit middle management and go back to being a reporter. Writing - not editing the writing of others – was, after all, my first love. I had made that clear to my supervisor and she said she'd keep it in mind, but nothing had happened for over a year.

So, I typed these words on a piece of paper:

I love my job. I make my living as a writer.

I enjoy my co-workers.

I tacked the paper on a wall in my cubicle. Every day I read those sentences, smiled and was thankful. There wasn't a doubt in my mind that I would achieve what I wanted and I practiced gratitude every day as if I'd already accomplished the goal.

Sure enough, a few months later there was a major reorganization at the newspaper and I became a writer. I would no longer be stuck in middle management, trying to please the people above and below me while I was miserable.

So many people were surprised by my decision because they considered it a demotion. Hardly! I had normal hours. I could spend more time with my teenage daughter. I got home in time to cook dinner. And I didn't have to supervise anyone. I was writing again, which is my passion and the reason I got into journalism. And my salary stayed the same. That, in my book, was a promotion!

To make matters even better, shortly after that, a job became available in the opinion section. The job would allow me to have my own column, something about which I'd always dreamed. So I applied along with several others.

Then I sat back and waited for my new boss to call and offer me the gig. I had claimed it and every day I thanked the Universe for giving it to me, never thinking for a moment the job would go to someone else.

A few weeks later I got that call and I got that job.

Now, I find something to be grateful for in every situation, even if it's nothing more than being thankful for the lesson. Everything that happens in our lives teaches us a lesson, even if we don't immediately see or understand it.

I used to lead a song in my church choir called *Be Grateful* by Walter Hawkins. It's a classic and one of my favorite gospel tunes.

No matter how bad we think things are in our lives, there is always someone else who has it worse. And there is always something about which to be grateful.

When we practice an attitude of gratitude, there's no room for anger. When we are busy being thankful for our abundance, we don't have time to find things about which to complain. If we really think about it, what are the benefits of complaining, anyway, other than attracting other complainers? You know, the whole misery loves company thing.

But gladness loves company, too!

I've never been particularly star struck, but I've come to believe that fascination with celebrities isn't about being in awe of them.

Everyone knows that the rich and the famous are no different from us. What celebrity watchers are fixated on is the happiness these people appear to have achieved through what they've accomplished. People who are star struck envy the lifestyles of the rich and famous, not the people themselves.

*Be grateful, because there's someone else who's worse off than you/Be grateful, because there's someone else who'd love to be in your shoes. ~ Walter Hawkins*

We love being in the company of people we define as successful, people we consider fun to be around. Angry, depressed people? People who do nothing but complain and gossip about others to make themselves feel superior? Not so much.

If you're one of those angry people, you'd have to admit that you don't much enjoy your own company, either. I know because I used to be one of them.

You will enjoy your own company a lot more when you cultivate gladness by choosing gratitude.

# LESSON #1

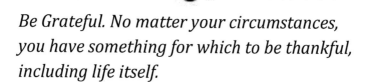

*Be Grateful. No matter your circumstances, you have something for which to be thankful, including life itself.*

## INNER WORK

### *BEING GRATEFUL*

What do you have to be grateful for?

Make a list of 10 things and find a place to put it where you will see it daily, perhaps, your bathroom.

Read the list every day, first thing in the morning and before you go to bed as a reminder to be grateful.

At least twice a week, take at least 10 minutes to meditate on your list.

You will find that when you are concentrating on the positive, the negative ceases to exist.

# Love's Got Everything To Do With It!

*~ To love oneself is the beginning of a life-long romance. ~ Oscar Wilde*

We are absolutely fascinated with love. It is the subject of countless songs, books, plays and movies. I think it's because so many people spend their lives searching for love, never truly understanding it.

Love gets the blame and credit for so much of what happens in society. People kill and die in its name. They subject themselves to abuse and put up with all manner of disrespect for what they believe is love. And they make inordinate sacrifices for it.

In *I Got Your Back: A Father and Son Keep It Real About Love, Fatherhood, Family, and Friendship*, singer Eddie Levert laments that had his son Gerald found love, he might not have died. Gerald had been in several relationships and had fathered several children, but had never found that one true love.

"His final album is called *In My Songs*," writes Eddie Levert. "In the title track he says, *"I want someone I can be lovey dovey with, I want someone that I can wake up with, I want someone that I can stroll through the park with, someone that I can be with like the ones I sing about in my songs...* I wanted him to find someone he trusted and believed in, someone who made him happy. The autopsy report cited that his death was due to a heart attack. I say my son really died of a broken heart, because he never met the woman he wanted, needed and really deserved."

That Eddie Levert wanted so much for his son to find that elusive loving relationship stayed with me long after I finished the book. Even though there are few love stories told from the male perspective, men long for love as much as women. They are just less emotional about it.

The universality of this dysfunction - seeking love outside ourselves – really struck me. This almost universal sense - even for the rich and famous like Gerald Levert - of being incomplete until we are in a love relationship haunts us.

We believe such a relationship will make us whole. That belief, however, is an illusion. Having a partner doesn't make us whole. We are born whole. And a mate doesn't give us love. It's something we already have. To find it, all we need to do is look within.

The search for love is really the search for self.

Love and joy are "inseparable from your natural state of inner connectedness with being," says author and spiritual teacher Eckhart Tolle in his book, *The Power of Now: A Guide to Spiritual Enlightenment.* "What is often referred to as love may be pleasurable and exciting for a while, but it is an addictive clinging, an extremely needy condition that can turn into its opposite at the flick of a switch."

I can clearly recall the day I defined my "addictive clinging" and "extremely needy condition" as love. I was sitting on my patio feeling extremely anxious because I had ended - for the umpteenth time - an unhealthy relationship with a man who had no plans to commit to me. I would get upset with him for lying to or disappointing me, which was often, and tell him it was over. Each time, he would convince me to give him another chance.

However, during the days between when I'd tell him it was over and when we'd actually see or talk to each other again, I'd be in misery wondering what would happen if it really was over. What if he took me at my word this time? How would my life change if I never saw him again? Would I be worse off than if I just kept dealing with his crap?

I'd be torn between knowing that I needed to let him go but not wanting to suffer through the loneliness of missing him. As I sat on the patio that evening staring into the darkness, I asked myself, Why do I always feel this way when it comes to letting this man go? My answer: I must be in love with him. How else could I explain it? Everything I knew about love I learned from books, magazines, movies, TV and the many dysfunctional relationships I'd observed. And what they taught me is that love is an emotion, overwhelming and consuming at times, and if a person can have that much of an effect on you – negatively or positively – it must be love. If you need that person and can't imagine your life without him or her – it must be love.

Looking back, of course, I know this isn't true. As Mr. Tolle says, "Real love doesn't make you suffer." But so many of us believe it does. If it doesn't hurt, it can't be love, right?

Wrong!

What we think is love - that feeling we have for that special someone who makes us feel like no other – more often than not is attachment. That's why when those special people don't behave the way we want them to, we get upset. We decide we don't like them or love them anymore because they haven't met our expectations. Then, suddenly we hate them. We want nothing to do with them.

This dysfunctional, emotional roller coaster ride is not love. Real love emanates from the soul. It is unconditional. It is our natural way of being. Real love allows others the freedom to be themselves.

Love doesn't depend on our mate or anyone else to be something for us that he or she is not and cannot be. It doesn't demand they be our savior or our source of happiness. Only we can save ourselves. We are our own rescuers. And only we can make ourselves happy because happiness comes from within. It's not a commodity for which we can make an exchange on the dating market.

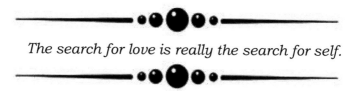

*The search for love is really the search for self.*

The illusion goes like this: If I wear just the right outfit and makeup, if I have the right job, income and personality, then I can attract that one person who will recognize my value and validate me. In exchange for giving of myself and all that I am, I will get what I need, which is for someone else to give me all of who they are. Then I will be complete.

The reality is unconditional love is accepting that we are where we're supposed to be. It means no regrets. Real love doesn't judge – ourselves or others. Accepting ourselves and others without judgment, accepting that we're all here on this planet to learn the same lessons; that is unconditional love.

Love isn't something we have to earn. We don't have to be worthy or good enough.

"You are the work of God, and His work is wholly lovable and wholly loving," says *A Course In Miracles*. "This is how a man must think of himself in his heart, because this is what he is."

Whether you believe in the God of Christianity, the God of Islam, the God of Judaism, a Universal God, a Higher Power, or no god at all, it's important to understand that you were born perfect and loving and lovable. Once we come into the knowledge that we are not here to find love, but that we in fact are love, that relationships are the vehicle through which we express that love, not acquire it, we then gain that peace that passeth all understanding. A woman at peace, one who is in love with herself, is a joy to be around. She attracts others who also are peaceful and loving.

Many sisters, though, have no idea what it really means to love ourselves. We hear all the time that if we don't love ourselves no one else will. But no one really tells us how to love ourselves. I've certainly never seen an instruction manual. Lacking a definition, we've depended on societal clues that lead us to believe that loving ourselves means having high self-esteem, self-respect and not letting someone walk all over us.

Some of us believe that we love ourselves by looking good. Black women spend an inordinate amount of money on their appearance – including $10 billion a year just on our hair!

But none of that gets us all the way there. Self-respect, self-esteem and great hair make us feel good about ourselves, but none of that gets us to love. Loving ourselves means being connected with our soul, our spirit. Recognizing that we were born perfect, not as sinners. That we are whole and complete, lacking nothing. That everything we need we already possess. That our strength comes from within, not from anger or pride. Or from someone else.

When we look for love outside ourselves, what we find are other people who also are seeking love outside themselves. The relationships that result are fraught with problems. How could we expect anything else? You have two people looking to each other to fulfill a need that can only be fulfilled by turning inward. We can't get love from someone else. We can only show love to someone else. The sooner we realize this, the happier we - and our romantic partners - will be.

Perhaps, Gerald Levert wouldn't have been so heartbroken had he realized that the love he sought was within.

I was sitting in my kitchen one day when the urge to write a poem hit me from nowhere. I love poetry and have written many poems and performed them for live audiences, but it had been years since I'd had a visit from my muse.

I grabbed my laptop and started typing and the following words just flowed:

*I have finally fallen in love.*
*With the perfect person, The One.*
*The One loves me exactly how I need to be loved.*
*Knows my every want and need and satisfies*
*each and every one of them.*
*The One doesn't judge me. Accepts me with all my*
*flaws. Understands that sometimes I get emotional*
*but doesn't take it personal. The One just smiles*
*and says, "She'll be alright if I just give her some*
*time."*
*The One encourages and supports me, let's me*
*know that I mean everything in the world and*
*everything will be alright.*
*I have been looking for this special someone all my*
*life. Never in my wildest dreams did I imagine that*
*one day I'd look in the mirror and see that she's*
*always been right here.*

You are all you need. Love yourself and the rest will follow.

# LESSON #2

*Love is within.*
*Do not seek love outside yourself.*

## INNER WORK

### *LOVING YOURSELF TRULY*

Find a picture of yourself as an infant. If you don't have one of yourself, find one of your child or someone else you love. Most of us see babies as perfectly innocent beings that we can love unconditionally. It's important to see ourselves that way so we can love ourselves unconditionally.

Meditate on the picture. See yourself as that child, loving and lovable. Recognize that the spirit that dwelled within you as a baby is exactly the same as the one within you today. The only thing that's changed is circumstances and experiences. You are just as lovable today as you were the day you were born.

Accept that you are where you are supposed to be. You are who you are supposed to be. Tell the child in the picture that you love her. Open your heart to her and realize you are opening your heart to yourself.

# Identity Crisis

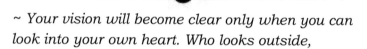

To become the grateful and loving women the Universe intended us to be, we first must discover our true identity. That means coming into the awareness that we are not our egos, we are not our thoughts, we are not our emotions, we are not our feelings, and we are not our personalities.

During the growing process from infancy to adulthood, we become identified with our personalities, our thoughts and beliefs, and the experiences that make up our lives. We define ourselves by these things and by the various roles we take on, including, mother, daughter, sister, lover, wife, and employee.

But our true identity is comprised of none of these things. It lies beyond that which we can see, touch, feel, taste or smell. And one day, we know.

Dancing to the Rhythm of My Soul

This awareness, or higher consciousness, is the realization that we are not human beings having an occasional spiritual experience. We are spiritual beings having a human experience.

This spiritual part of our being, to most of us, is a stranger. Yet, this spirit, soul, or whatever you wish to label it, is the essence of who we really are.

The soul, in many religions and philosophical traditions, denotes the immortal inner essence. Christianity, the faith of my family, teaches that God saves the souls of those who seek forgiveness of their sins and obey Him.

Those special people who obey His word – the saints – will go to heaven where they will live forever. Sinners, those who break the rules, will go to hell where they will burn for eternity.

Muslims believe that we must live this life in a way that pleases Allah so that after we die we can go to Paradise.

But what about this life? If you're like me, you want freedom from the negative thoughts, emotions and experiences that so often make this life, this time period, hell on earth. I want heaven now. I don't want to wait until the hereafter.

The good news is that I can have it now and so can you. We don't have to suffer now to earn the reward of peace and happiness after we die. Peace and happiness come when we connect with our spirit. This inner connectedness brings about enlightenment. The state of enlightenment empowers us to move beyond thoughts, emotions, and events because it is the realization that the external is a reflection of the internal. We can change the outer by changing the inner. We no longer have to be victims of circumstances.

It is in the state of enlightenment that we recognize that we are the author, director and producer of our lives. The choices that we make – whether conscious or unconscious – determine what happens in the next scene, the next chapter. The decision we must make is whether we want our lives to unfold consciously – at a higher level of awareness - or unconsciously – at a lower level of awareness.

To choose the lower level is to be observers of our life events much like moviegoers watching a film. Yet, because most of us are unaware, this is exactly how we live our lives. We are in a constant state of reaction. Reacting to the outside world and its people, places, things and events because in the absence of awareness they have control over us.

Reacting means to behave as we have always done – re-acting. Our actions are automatic, on auto pilot so to speak, because they are controlled by our past experiences, by what we already know. My mother disciplined by yelling at my four siblings and me. My sister and I disciplined our children by yelling. It's what we knew based on our past experiences. My children have told me that the one major fault they believe I had as a parent was that I yelled too much. They say I acted like a crazy person. As I look in the rear view mirror of my life and recall certain scenes – such as the times I screamed like a hyena because the trash didn't get taken out or the dishes weren't done – I can see their point.

I used to tell them that they were the reason why I yelled so much because they often disobeyed me by not doing their chores. Today, I understand that the only thing that affects me is me. How I choose to handle certain situations is on me. No one else can force me to yell. I could just as easily have chosen to sit my children down and express my frustration using my inside voice.

I don't doubt that I would've gotten a much more positive response. As I became more enlightened and realized that I was living the definition of insanity – doing the same thing over and over and expecting something different – I realized I needed to stop reacting, and start responding. Responding means to assess a situation from the only place that makes sense, the only place where we have power, and to act accordingly. That place is the present moment.

Since neither the past nor the future exists, we are powerless to act from either place. It's far easier to stay present when we are connected to our spirit. Then we are in control. We know we're connected because there is an absence of pain and anger. When we are present, we're not dwelling on the past or fretting over the future. We feel joy. We go with the flow. There is no resistance. We accept things as they are because we know that's exactly how they are supposed to be. We are at peace.

I read a story once about a girl who had a disease that caused her excruciating pain. The doctors tried everything to give her relief, but no medicine worked. What did work was reading. The girl found that when she read, the pain disappeared.

How on earth can reading stop pain? I wondered. Then it hit me. When she reads she is present. She is in the moment. Like a laser beam, her attention focuses on the printed words. There is no attention left to concentrate on the pain. So the pain no longer exists.

Concentrating our attention in one place like this makes us present. Whether it be reading, writing, jogging, making jewelry, or working out, each of us has something we love to do in which we lose ourselves. Our ego selves.

We may not realize that's what happening, but it happens nonetheless.

For Omar that something is riding his motorcycle. He likes to take long scenic routes where the only sound he hears is the engine of his bike. As he was telling me one day how much he enjoyed it, I asked him why he thought that was. He couldn't explain it. "Because it puts you," I told him, "in the present."

"Wow," he said. "I never thought about it like that, but you're right."

Omar never thought about it like that because he doesn't try to stay present intentionally. It just happens.

He rides because he enjoys the serenity, the absence of thoughts invading his mind like daggers. He didn't realize that this was presence or that it could take him to a higher level of consciousness.

For many of us connecting to our inner essence, our spirit, is difficult because we find it so hard to purposefully disconnect from our minds. The mind may be a terrible thing to waste, but it's also a place where we waste far too much time and energy. We are slaves to our minds. The mind controls everything we do. How we interpret the events of our lives depends on our state of mind. The state of our minds is dictated by our personal histories. In other words, the mind defines our reality. And the mind is filled with illusions.

The mind analyzes, justifies, rationalizes and makes up theories. Have you ever noticed how difficult it is to empty your mind of thoughts? To turn off that voice in your head and enjoy complete silence? Have you ever had an argument with yourself in your head? There are days when my mind is a battlefield of warring thoughts.

People often say that their mind is playing tricks on them. It does.

If we hear something often enough, we eventually start to believe it, regardless of whether it has any basis in fact. How else do you explain the birthers – people who believe President Barack Obama wasn't born in the United States, despite the availability at the click of a mouse of his Hawaiian birth certificate?

That's how the mind works. It's always on repeat, replaying the same thoughts over and over until we believe them. Then act on them.

I first became aware of the mind's power to deceive one night when I was trying to comprehend the unpredictable and inconsiderate behavior of the man in my life. I concluded, with not one shred of evidence, that he must have been seeing another woman. That was the only thing that made sense, according to my mind. The more I contemplated this thought – this theory constructed by my mind – the angrier I became. My heart began to race. My breaths shortened. I had convinced myself that he was a liar and with all the righteous indignation I could muster, I jumped out of bed and went searching for my cell phone so I could call and cuss him out.

Dancing to the Rhythm of My Soul

Thankfully, before I dialed the number, I came to my senses. I realized that I had no idea whatsoever if my theory was true, yet I was prepared to act on it as though it were gospel. Even if my theory were true, that phone call wasn't going to do anything but make me even angrier and make him think that I had lost my mind.

We're told this is what mentally ill people do – act on delusions created in the mind. We may not talk about it, but the rest of us do it, too.

To uncover our true identity we must take a vacation from our mind. One way to do that is to step back and watch our mind and its thoughts. I've done this during my morning shower and found myself laughing at the way thoughts bombard my psyche one after the other, each vying for attention. As I inhaled vanilla scented body wash and then massaged a soap soaked sponged across my arms and chest, I waited for the next thought to come and realized it was the exact same thought I'd had in the shower the day before. And the day before that.

These thoughts don't create. They frustrate. The epiphany for me is that I am not my mind and its incessant repetitive thoughts, but I am the watcher of my mind.

So losing my mind isn't necessarily a bad thing. The ability to escape from the voice in our head, to pull our concentration from the endless stream of repetitive thoughts and to focus that attention deep within is what gets us to peace. When the mind becomes silent, we can experience inner connectedness. We create space to commune with our souls and understand that we are not our thoughts. We don't have to let them control us.

This inner awakening, which is by no means an overnight process for most of us, is what it means to find ourselves. Not the ego self that the events of our lives have molded us into, but our authentic selves.

Some spiritual teachers call that entity the observer. Have you ever noticed that when you're dreaming, there's a part of you who knows that you're dreaming? That's the observer. The real you. The One.

The you that is immortal and is not affected by what happens outside of yourself. The you that never changes. The observer that recognized when you were dreaming 10 years ago is the same observer that recognized you were dreaming last night.

Our personalities change based on what happens over the course of the time we spend here on earth. And our bodies change to reflect that time. Even our minds change as we have new experiences and create new thoughts. Our souls, our spirits, however, never change.

# Dancing to the Rhythm of My Soul

Spirituality enhances our human life experience. It gives us a greater sense of meaning and purpose. We are at our most creative when we are connected to our spirit. We are our most powerful selves. Our most positive selves. Our most peaceful selves. Our happiest selves. We are problem free. We are one with the Universe.

I find it easiest to connect with my inner self by meditating and by communing with nature.

I will go for a swim first thing in the morning or late at night when I can have the pool all to myself. I float on my back and focus on the sky. In daylight, I lose myself – my ego self - watching as the rays of the sun dance on the water, surrounding me with liquid diamonds. Or in the sway of the palm tree leaves as the wind plays them like an accordion.

At night, I lose myself – my ego self – under the blanket of the black sky and its twinkling stars. With ears under water the only sound I can hear is that of my own breathing. I recognize that I am one with the stars, the moon, the sun, and the trees. One with the sky, the wind and the blades of grass.

I find myself - my soul self - when I stay in the moment and recognize that I am one with the Universe. This is consciousness. It is here where I find out who I am and have always been.

It is in those moments when I am able to silence my mind that problems disappear. Fear is non-existent. The past and future have no meaning. What other people think about me doesn't matter. I take nothing personally.

This is the peace that passeth all understanding. What happens externally has no effect on me internally. I know that who I truly am is beyond my circumstances, beyond my thoughts and beyond the events that unfold in my life.

All that exists is my perfect soul-self and all is perfectly right in my world. I have heaven on earth.

I am pure awareness. I am that I am. And so are you.

# LESSON #3

*Know your true identity.*
*You are a spiritual being in a physical,*
*human body.*

## INNER WORK

### *TO KNOW THYSELF*
### *IS TO LOVE THYSELF*

Find a quiet spot where you can avoid the distraction of sounds. Close your eyes and empty your mind of thoughts.

Embrace the silence and focus your attention within. Breathe deeply and focus your attention on your breath. If thoughts come, let them pass through and then dismiss them. Don't indulge them or resist them. Resisting only ensures that they hang around longer.

Experience the calmness, the expanse of consciousness and the peace. This is the real you.

Do this often as it keeps you calm and centered and helps you deal with life's challenges.

# From Diva to Divine

*~ You are here to realize your inner divinity and manifest your innate enlightenment. ~ Morihei Ueshiba*

You can learn a lot from the movies. When Neo in the 1999 Warner Brothers film, The Matrix, realized that he was The One, there was that memorable moment when he stood up, his body riddled with bullet holes, put up his hand and said, "No." A hail of bullets fell harmlessly to the ground.

He didn't develop superpowers. Neo was the same man: just as invincible in that moment as he'd been five minutes earlier, five hours earlier, even five years earlier. But he hadn't known he was invincible. As a result, the bad guys were able to kill him. Love and an unshakeable belief in a prophecy allowed him to rise from the dead, vanquish the bad guys and save the world.

When we become aware of our true identity, we, too, become invincible. We realize that we are beyond divas. We are divine.

Divas identify with their personality. And that's fine. Our personalities make us the unique individual human beings that we are. But our spirit makes us the spiritual beings that we are.

Divine women identify with their spirit.

What's important is being able to distinguish between the two. When we identify with our spirit, we know that we are invincible. Like Jesus, we are here on earth for only a certain number of days during which we occupy a human body. One day, that body will cease to exist. But the spirit that dwells within never dies.

That awareness abolishes fear and gives us a huge sense of power. That power gives us the ability to stop emotional bullets with our hands. Bullets like insecurity, low self-esteem, fear of abandonment. Bullets like addiction, jealousy, neediness, unforgiveness and destructive anger have the power to kill. Riddled with these bullets, we are not truly living. We are existing. We are powerless.

When we can live free from fear and all that accompanies fear, we have immeasurable power. As the Bible says in Isaiah 54:17, "No weapon that is formed against thee shall prosper." If no weapon has power over you, aren't you invincible? Doesn't that make you The One?

When we recognize our divinity, we are fearless because we know nothing can hurt us. Our bodies - that outer shell that dwells in time and space and has an expiration date - can experience pain, but not our spirit. Not our eternal essence.

In 2001, the prestigious medical journal, The Lancet, published a study by a Dutch cardiologist who has become convinced there is life after death – perhaps better described as life after life. Dr. Pim van Lommel, author of *Consciousness, The Science of the Near Death Experience*, came to this belief following a research project he conducted on heart patients. Of 344 people who had survived cardiac arrest, sixty two -18 percent - reported a near death experience. They recalled a state of consciousness during which they had an out-of-body experience. Usually, they saw a tunnel, a light and deceased relatives. Many had what Dr. van Lommel calls a "life review," during which the events of their lives played out before them like a movie. They reported feeling safe and protected.

After being resuscitated and resuming their earthly lives, they reported becoming more spiritual, more compassionate toward themselves and others, and more connected to the world around them.

What fascinated Dr. van Lommel was the fact that during these experiences the patients were all clinically dead. There was no blood flow to the brain. How could any level of consciousness exist if there was no brain function? If the brain isn't functioning there's no way a person could have any experience much less remember it. Or could they?

Apparently they could. Patients who had a near death experience told Dr. van Lommel that the dimension in which they found themselves was far more real than anything they'd ever experienced. "They tell us," he said, "'I felt home. It's where I come from.'"

In an interview with Mel van Dusen, producer of Present!, a California-based cable television show, Dr. van Lommel said the patients no longer feared death and had different values. "What is important in life," he said they learned, "is unconditional love and acceptance and compassion toward yourself and others and nature."

The research project also changed the doctor's life. He quit working as a cardiologist to focus his attention full time on the study of consciousness.

It will probably take the medical community some time to accept the fact that humans are not just biological beings, but also divine, spiritual beings. It's a big leap for a scientist to accept that the death of the body does not mean death of the soul.

When I connect with my inner spirit, however, I know it without a doubt. I am without worry or fear. I am totally and completely at peace. When challenges arise, I look at them as lessons instead of problems. I resist the urge to judge myself. (I'm not always successful, we are works in progress!) I try and figure out what the lesson is I'm supposed to learn from the experience. I tell myself that, this, too, shall pass. And everything will be OK because it always is. And everything does become OK.

One of the greatest challenges to come my way occurred when my mother lost her second leg to peripheral artery disease. Though she lives in Massachusetts, she was staying with me in Florida at the time. I can replay in my mind like a human DVD player the scene in which I discussed her condition with a vascular surgeon. The doctor, whom I was meeting for the first time, told me in a very matter of fact way that even if he were able to remove the clot that was causing the problem and save her leg that I should not expect my mother to live as independently as she had before that night.

My mother has lived her life for other people as long as I can remember; her children, her grandchildren, the students at the various schools where she's worked have been her life. She was the rock of our family, always there for everyone else. She's been a pillar in the community, a second mother to her nieces and nephews. She's a mother figure to the children in the neighborhood.

It was bad enough that she had endured a stroke twenty years earlier that had put her in a wheelchair with only two working limbs, one leg and one arm. Still, after working hard in physical therapy she managed to live alone and work part time, running a breakfast program for public school students. She devoted herself to that job. She spent her own money to sponsor magic tray days and events, during which she gave prizes to the kids. She bought them gloves and found them jackets and boots, because so many of the children came to school in the winter wearing flip flops. They had no winter shoes or a winter coat. My mother isn't a saint, but she's about as close to it as anyone I've met in my lifetime.

Now, she was in danger of losing another limb! Anger attached itself to me like a magnet. How could life be so damned unfair? Hadn't she gone through enough? Of all people, why should something like this happen to her?

After the vascular surgeon disappeared behind the oak doors that led to the operating room, I lost it. Anger and fear put my gut in a vice grip and choked the air from my lungs. I threw my purse and the latte I'd been holding during our conversation at a wall and howled so loudly the staff came running. By the time the nurses appeared at my side, I was doubled over against the wall, tears raining down my face. If there was a God, I thought, He was no damned friend of mine.

My mother emerged from the surgery and remained in the hospital for what seemed like a lifetime. During the fight to save her leg she contracted a hospital-acquired infection that worsened her already fragile condition. She stopped eating, dropping more than 100 pounds. She told me she didn't have the energy to fight. She was ready to go home to be with the Lord. She was released from the hospital to a nursing home for rehabilitation only to return to the hospital several times because of seizures and infections. And in the end, she lost the leg.

As this ordeal unfolded, I had to hold down a full time job, parent my teenage daughter, and spend as much time as possible at the various hospitals and the nursing home. And I had to be vigilant about my mother's care; educating myself about the myriad medications she'd been prescribed to ensure that the medical professionals didn't kill her with their so-called cures.

I had to come to terms with the possibility that the ending to this drama could very well be my mother's funeral. She was still alive, but our thoughts and fears are powerful enough to make the unreal very real for us. When I pictured her dead, the feelings that accompanied that image were overwhelming.

One night, the reality of my mother's immortality slapped me across the face. I was driving home from the last of the three Florida hospitals where she'd served time when suddenly the oxygen in my car evaporated. I gasped for air and felt my stomach churning as I struggled to comprehend the fact that she might actually die. It's not as if I had expected her to live forever. I'd gone through similar feelings when she'd had the stroke twenty years earlier. This was different. She was much older this time. And she'd given up. I pulled over to the side of the road, caught my breath and then released it in a scream that could wake my ancestors.

I knew I couldn't fall apart. My mother needed me. My daughter needed me, too. My brothers and sister in Massachusetts needed daily updates on her condition and reassurance that she would be alright. And I had to maintain my job.

I got through by remembering who I am. And by remembering who my mother is. We are spiritual beings having a natural experience. And though my mother will one day leave her body, she will never truly leave me. We both are one with the same Universe.

If my mother was indeed ready to leave this earth, I had to let her go. I couldn't try to force her to stay here with me so that I could feel better. It helped tremendously to know that her death would not be the end of her.

The response to a column I wrote about making peace with my mother's mortality was one of my most rewarding experiences as a writer. So many people who had lost a loved one or whose loved ones were terminally ill reached out to tell me how much the column had helped them, including a doctor whose mother was in hospice care. The doctor told me that my column had inspired her to do for her mother what I had become willing to do for mine: love her enough to let her go in her own way.

Here is the column:

*Dear Mom,*

*Today is Good Friday, the day Christians recall the crucifixion of Jesus Christ.*

*As you endure your own personal torture, I can't help but recall your statement to me earlier this week. "I want to go home to be with the Lord."*

*I want you to know I understand.*

*You're tired. You don't have the will to fight. And I realize now that I can't fight for you.*

*You no longer want to deal with the medications, the needles, the IVs, the rotation of strangers -- many of them cold and aloof -- in and out of your room telling you what to do. Or your grown children shoving food and water at you though you clearly have no desire to eat.*

*I'd love to see you enjoy one of your favorite fish dinners, but you're just not in the mood. I can't even coax you with the candy bars and ice cream I used to chastise you for eating so much of. "Not right now," you say, "maybe later."*

*But later never comes.*

*I have to be OK with that because it's your right to choose when and what you eat. How you want to live. And how you want to die.*

*"I can't," you said, "go to glory as a coward."*

*A woman who alone raised five children into adulthood successfully is no coward. A woman who survived a stroke and figured out a way to live independently with one leg and one arm is no coward. A woman who responds from her hospital bed, "She lived a wonderful life," to the question of what she wants written on her tombstone is no coward. Many people can't even talk about the inevitable, but you are willing.*

*No, Mom, you're no coward. You're simply exhausted.*

*I want you to know that whatever you choose to do, I'll support your decision.*

*If you decide to fight, I'll be in your corner wiping the sweat from your golden brow that carries not a single wrinkle. When you need to cry, I will wipe your tears. I could never do for you all that you've done for me. But I will do all that I can.*

*If you decide it's time to transition, I will help you on your journey and find a way to let you go. Though I cannot even begin to imagine my life without you, I will not try to keep you here for my own selfish reasons.*

*I will no longer force you to do anything you don't want. I'll never forget the look on your face when you asked, "Why did you let them cut me open?"*

Dancing to the Rhythm of My Soul

*You told me not to let them, but I thought I was doing what's best. I'm sorry.*

*It's your life, and from now on, it's your decision. I promise.*

*I know that you're not -- in your words -- a "dingbat!"*

*What you are is a woman who has given much, taken little, and who has made the world a better place for all those for whom she loves and cares.*

*My greatest wish is that you find peace of mind. You often tell me that I don't know what you're going through. You're right. I have no idea. I can only sympathize and empathize. I do know, though, that peace of mind is a tremendous blessing that you could use right now.*

*I hope knowing that your children will respect your choices and will be proud of you, no matter what, helps you find that peace.*

*As my sister and I prepare to take you home to fulfill your wish of being in your church this Easter surrounded by your children and grandchildren to celebrate the Resurrection, I take solace knowing that death could never truly take you from me. You are a part of me.*

My mother fought her way through this ordeal and, with help, is blessed to be able to live at home instead of a nursing home. When that time really does come for me to say goodbye to my parents, or when my time here comes to an end, I will be able to let go much more easily now, knowing that it will not be the end of us.

We are divine.

# LESSON #4

*You are more than your personality and the sum total of your life experiences. You are an immortal soul.*

## INNER WORK

### *CONNECTING WITH YOUR DIVINITY*

Create a private space in your home and fill it with the beautiful things that make you happy, such as pictures of your favorite people and favorite things, stuffed animals, cherished gifts or cards from loved ones.

Make this a peaceful place. Include your favorite scents such as potpourri, incense or scented candles.

Make time to visit this space often. Meditate there. Bask in the feelings that the items and scents bring you. Play your favorite meditation or similar music that soothes you.

Spending time in this place will bring you serenity and that will bring you closer to the divinity within.

You also can set aside time each week to do your favorite hobby, that special thing you do that takes your mind off everything else and puts you in the present.

# Forgive to Live

*~ To forgive is to set a prisoner free and discover that the prisoner was you. ~ Lewis B. Smedes*

The voice on the television filled the room but it could have been speaking Italian for all the attention I was paying. My mind was in the future, floating atop the clouds I knew I'd soon see on my flight back to Massachusetts.

I was in a North Carolina hotel room decompressing from a day of interviews at the News & Observer in Raleigh. They'd flown me in to apply for an editing job. It was my second interview at a newspaper other than my hometown daily where I'd worked for 12 years. I was desperate to leave Springfield for a number of reasons, not the least of which was my job.

As I lay in the hotel bed wondering how much longer I could stand the Union-News and the city where I'd spent my life, my past suddenly flashed through my mind like lightning in a dark sky.

The epiphany that followed informed me that I needed more than a new job and a new zip code to get a new life. In addition to feeling claustrophobic in the city where I spent my youth and fast approaching middle age, I was miserable working for a newspaper that I felt didn't live up to my journalistic standards. Mentally and emotionally, I was stuck on pause. What hit me in the still moment in that hotel room was that I couldn't fast forward because I'd been subconsciously holding on to a mountain of guilt and shame - the residue of my past mistakes.

I'd gone to the altar at church numerous times and had asked for God's forgiveness. I believed that He had responded in the affirmative. Still, I found it difficult not to beat myself up and live in the past where those mistakes resided. What I've come to learn is that the past doesn't exist. Nothing can take place there. If we're stuck in the past – trapped by our uncreative thoughts - we can't create anything new. We certainly can't create a new life.

To create something new requires letting go of the guilt and shame that is the glue that keeps us stuck in the past. That means forgiving ourselves.

Having God's forgiveness – if we believe in God – is great. Having our own forgiveness is even greater. That discovery led me that night to pen this poem:

## I FORGIVE ME

*I forgive me....*
*For the choices I've made that hurt me*
*For the decisions I knew were wrong*
*For the love I gave to those unworthy*
*For taking paths on which I didn't belong*
*I let go of the guilt for not making better choices*
*For being naive, for closing my eyes, for settling for less*
*For not heeding my own advice and listening to other voices,*
*And allowing them to lead to me to places I'd never guess*
*I forgive me and let it go; I make peace with my past*
*Knowing that I can now take full control of my life*
*No longer stuck on rewind, I can press forward fast*
*And bury all the misery, heartache, pain, and strife*
*It will not be forgotten, though, I will use it to remind me*
*To learn from my mistakes and be proud of who I've become*
*Someone loving and strong who has matured enough to see*
*That my future is what I make it and not determined by where I came from*

*And that future will be a bright one, because it's in my hands*

*I've come into my own and I won't settle for just anything*

*I deserve the best and anything less isn't in my plans*

*For I'm entitled to all the good that life can bring*

Once we forgive ourselves, we then can forgive others. Not as a favor to those who've hurt us, but to free ourselves from that hurt and the destructive power it exerts over our lives.

So many of us hold on to anger towards others for fear that letting go of anger means letting them off the hook. We want them to feel the same pain we do. If we let it go, how will they pay for what they did to us?

The problem with that thinking is that we are the ones who end up paying. Holding on to anger and bitterness keeps us from fulfilling our potential. It keeps us from our joy. We are the ones who end up paying for their transgression over and over while they live their lives, often with no thought or care about us.

It took Carla many years to understand that she needed to forgive her ex-husband for cheating on her and robbing her of the family she'd always wanted. Carla insisted that she wasn't bitter. She was scarred. So badly that she didn't believe she would ever love another man as much as she loved Peter.

A scar, though, is what's left behind after an injury heals. It is evidence that something bad happened. It also is evidence that things heal and that life goes on. So, if we don't forgive those who inflict emotional injury upon us, we don't heal and unconsciously we still suffer from the pain.

Carla believed that she had moved on. She relocated to a new city, got a new job and started a new life. That years later she couldn't discuss forgiving Peter without getting angry and raising her voice, though, meant the ghosts of the past had followed Carla to her new address.

Eventually, she came to understand that Peter was happily living his life with his second wife and family. He wasn't the least bit affected by the fact that she hadn't forgiven him. The only person affected was Carla. And she was the only person who could do something about it.

My capacity to give and receive love increased exponentially after I forgave my father for leaving our family and neglecting to stay involved in my life. It was a resentment that I carried for years, but about which I wasn't even aware.

I can still clearly recall the day he left. My mother was in her nightgown on the stairs crying and begging him not to go. My siblings and I were crying, too. I was eight. My youngest brother at the time was three. With a single brown suitcase, my father walked out the door in the midst of all the wailing and never lived with us as a family again.

He'd pick the five of us up every now and then and even kept us for a summer when he lived in Wisconsin. But even then, he was rarely there, leaving us in the care of his mother or his sister.

He was notorious for making promises that he didn't keep and was absent from our lives except for holidays and family reunions. I thought that I had made peace with the situation and had accepted him for the person that he was until a light clicked on one Thanksgiving Day. It was the first with my dad that I could recall since he left. He spent Thanksgivings with his wife's family in New Jersey and Christmas in Springfield with both his family and hers. This was my first ever Thanksgiving with my stepmother and my youngest sister.

I got extremely angry with my dad that day when he seemed to be taking my sister's side in an argument. The intensity of my anger surprised me. It seemed to come from nowhere. I later realized these unearthed feelings were the result of the resentment that I held against my father for having a closer relationship with my sister and her child than he did with me and my children. In my adult mind, I know that's what usually happens when a man leaves one family and takes on another. But in the heart and mind of the child within, it was rejection, plain and simple. That child believed my dad had made a conscious decision to choose his other family instead of me.

It became clear that the feelings of abandonment, neglect, and unworthiness I thought I'd let go of two decades earlier had only been buried alive, hiding in a place so deep I didn't see their impact on my choices. Chief among those choices were the men I had allowed into my life.

I thought I had rotten luck with men and never could figure out why good men rarely crossed my path. On the rare occasions they did, I was never attracted to them for some reason or another.

It hit me that Thanksgiving Day: because I didn't expect to meet a good man, I didn't meet one. And the reason I didn't expect one was the dysfunctional, even non-existent relationship I'd had with the man who was supposed to be my first love.

Of course, this isn't news to most women who've had similar stories with their fathers. But I don't think that most of us are aware of just how important it is to forgive them. Nor are we aware of how our thoughts and beliefs, which are based on the character of that relationship – determine our reality. It determines our expectations.

I once dated a guy who told me that I didn't act like I wanted to be in a relationship. comment came as a surprise because that wasn't true. I did want to be in a relationship. I know now that I was responsible for the mistaken impression he had of me. I didn't trust men so I was guarded and defensive. I'd built an almost impenetrable wall around myself.

Because I expected disappointment, I usually got exactly what I expected. I didn't, however, realize any of that on a conscious level.

Subconsciously, I had tried to insulate myself emotionally to keep from getting hurt. But eventually something always happened that would stir that pain buried in my internal vault. It always found ways of escaping. Sometimes it surfaced as anger. Other times it appeared as controlling behavior. Pain takes on whatever form the ego feels necessary to preserve itself, because pain feeds the ego. Once we relinquish pain through forgiveness, our ego weakens and our spirit grows.

I was able to release my anger and resentment by forgiving my dad. Once I recognized my deep seated resentment toward my father, I confronted him and we agreed to talk.

We wrote each other letters first, putting all our cards on the table. Then we had dinner. I came to understand that my father really didn't know how to parent. At the time, he was incapable of putting others before himself.

I don't believe my dad made a conscious decision to ignore his children. He just did what he wanted to do without regard for the impact his behavior would have on us. He did it unconsciously. Most of us don't hurt others consciously. And even if my dad did know what he was doing, I still had to forgive him for my sake.

Forgiving someone for a real or perceived hurt is liberating. As long as we harbor ill feelings toward that person he or she holds power over us. While we're busy being offended, the objects of our anger are going about their business living their lives and feeling just fine!

*Holding on to grudges and resentments makes us weak and reduces our ability to give and receive love. Forgiveness is empowering and increases our capacity for love.*

We must forgive ourselves first. Then, as difficult as it may be, we have to forgive others. It's been said that forgiving a friend is harder than forgiving an enemy. That makes sense. We don't expect our friends or the people we love to cause us pain. We expect that from our enemies. Yet, as hard as it may be to forgive our parents, our families, our friends, we have to do so. We have to forgive our spouses, lovers, ex-spouses and ex-lovers. We have to forgive our bosses, co-workers, friends and former friends.

Any time we are holding on to resentment against anyone in our life, we are holding on to negative energy that holds us back and takes up room where joy could live.

We don't have to forget, but if we want to be truly free, we have to forgive.

# LESSON #5

*Forgiveness is the key to happiness. Only when you forgive – yourself and others – can you truly move forward with your life and grow as a person.*

# INNER WORK

## *FORGIVING TO GET ON WITH LIVING*

Make a list of everyone in your life, including yourself, whom you need to forgive and for what. Go down that list and visualize each person. Say aloud, "I forgive you. I know you did the best you could at your level of awareness."

If you want, you can also write a letter to each of these people. Mail the letter if you want to, but realize it's not important that these people know that you have forgiven them. It's only important that you know you have forgiven them. Actually writing these letters is cathartic. You will find it is a healing release. Those individuals will no longer have power over you. When you are done, burn the list and the letters or simply throw them away as a symbol that you are now done holding on to these resentments. Some people will be easier to forgive than others so doing this once may not be enough.

Repeat this process as many times as necessary to truly feel that you have let go of all the negative emotions that you are holding toward each person on your list, including yourself.

# Being the Change
# You Want to See

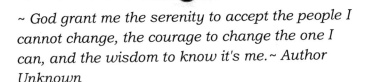

*~ God grant me the serenity to accept the people I cannot change, the courage to change the one I can, and the wisdom to know it's me.~ Author Unknown*

I will never forget the first time I became aware of my power to transform the environment around me. It's a power we all possess: being the change we want to see.

"Be the change you want to see:" it's a quote from Buddha that's thrown around a lot, but how often do we actualize it? The first time I made it a reality was totally unintentional.

I had just finished Gary Zukav's *Seat of the Soul*, the book that set me on my journey toward spiritual fulfillment. I had decided that the first of several areas of my life I would work on was patience. It's a virtue of which I was in short supply. As I looked back, I could see there were many mistakes I could have avoided had I had more.

Once you identify the issues you want to address in your life, believe me, the Universe will cooperate by sending you many challenges in those areas! My first big challenge came at an Albertson's grocery store. I was on my way to the gym and decided to pick up something for lunch. When my grapes rang up higher than the sale price listed in the produce department, I asked the cashier to honor the lower price. That's when the drama began.

When the cashier put the grapes on the scale to void the erroneous price, somehow they weighed less than when she rang them up! For a good 10 minutes, the cashier tried everything to get the grapes to weigh the same. She put a grocery bag on them. Then a pack of gum. A piece of paper. Nothing worked. Soon, a second clerk arrived on the scene. She couldn't figure out how to solve the problem, either. All the while, I just stood there and smiled. Inside I was shaking like a smoker having a nicotine fit, but on the outside I was as cool as a fall day in New England. I was determined to practice patience.

A third clerk arrived, and she was just as baffled. By this time, I regretted ever asking for the price change. It was only 50 cents a pound! Finally, after 20 minutes, I suggested that the Three Stooges void the entire sale and start over.

One of them looked at me as though I had asked for her first born!

The old Rhonda was fuming inside. I was exhibiting the patience of Job while being inconvenienced and she had the attitude?

The old Rhonda was ready. She knew just what to say. "Who the hell are you giving attitude lady!? Haven't you heard that the customer is always right? I'm the one who should be pissed waiting all day for the three of you geniuses to figure out how to void one freakin' bag of grapes. Maybe one of you can figure out how to cancel the whole damn sale so I can get to the gym where I should've been 15 minutes ago!"

The old Rhonda would have stormed out, leaving the food on the conveyer belt!

Instead, I smiled and waited another five minutes for the brain trust to come up with a solution. Then, once again I suggested they ring my four items all over again. That idea was vetoed.

I smiled again, telling myself that if I could get through this without losing it, I would emerge a much more patient and better person.

Just then, I looked around and noticed there were at least eight people waiting in line behind me where there had been none. One of the cashiers now huddled around my register had originally come on the floor to open another register. Even seeing the line that had developed -

and despite the fact that she was being of no use solving the mystery of the grapes – she didn't bother to open her register to relieve the line that had formed.

What I found amazing was the patience of those customers. They were perusing magazines, sending texts, or standing and doing nothing. All of them were just calmly waiting. Nothing on their faces or in their demeanor indicated they were the least little bit annoyed. I was in shock. There was no agitation, no fidgeting. No demands for the cashiers to speed things up or get a manager!

And then it occurred to me that they were calm because I was. Had I been sighing, sucking my teeth, demanding a manager intervene with the trio of cashiers, or showing any other of my usual signs of impatience, I have no doubt those waiting behind me would have picked up on and amplified that negative energy. I can't count the number of times I've been waiting in a slow moving line when one person's complaining was all it took for everyone else in the line to join in. Within moments, you've got a line full of agitated, impatient customers.

The fact that I stayed calm – with a smile on my face no less – meant the other customers stayed that way, too. By being the change I wanted to see in myself – patient – I effected that change in those around me.

# Dancing to the Rhythm of My Soul

In the end, the cashier who had twice refused my request to redo the entire sale decided it was the only thing to do after all! By then, I only had enough time to shower and dress at the gym. I had to skip my workout and go straight to the office. I'm not pretending I wasn't irritated. But the lesson I learned in that store about my own control of my reality was invaluable.

It has helped tremendously in all areas of my life, particularly in relationships.

Not long after that grocery store episode, the man I was dating suddenly stopped communicating with me. For several days I got no calls or texts, and he wouldn't return mine.

Over the course of those days I went from feeling disrespected, neglected and rejected to just plain mad. I was obsessed with trying to figure out what could take him from one extreme – calling several times a day and lavishing me with attention – to another – totally ignoring me.

I finally decided that I couldn't make sense out of nonsense so I stopped trying. But that didn't make me really feel any better. Then one morning at the gym, with thoughts of him disturbing my peace of mind and slowing down my workout, I got a moment of clarity. I realized that I needed to stop being mad and find a way to get glad. That doesn't sound like much of an epiphany, but it was. It dawned on me that only I could control how I felt. I was responsible for how I interpreted his behavior and the impact I let it have on me. Up until then, I had been putting all the blame for my misery on him. I had given him total control and responsibility for my emotions. By doing that, I had become paralyzed, unable to free myself from the negativity that was eating away at me. Meanwhile, he was going about his merry way!

I had to decide what the best outcome for me would be. Let go of the anger, forget about him, and move on? Or let go of the anger and figure out how to get the response from him I wanted?

I went with the latter. After all, what I was most upset about was the sudden absence of him from my life. I missed him. Sure, my ego was telling me to be offended by his behavior. The ego loves having that negative energy to feed on. Me? Not so much. I find it exhausting and emotionally debilitating.

So, I decided to send him a romantic text, the kind any man would be happy to get. The other messages I'd been sending were either needy or nasty, depending on whether I was feeling lonely or angry at the time. It's no wonder I didn't get a response!

This message came from a confident, aware woman. Desire replaced desperation. Assuredness replaced anger. Naughty replaced needy!

I got exactly the response I wanted and eventually we saw each other again and I got an explanation for his behavior. At that point, though, the explanation didn't really matter.

What had become more important was the discovery that I could choose not to let his behavior twist my insides into knots. Since I can't change him – or anyone else for that matter – I have to turn the camera on myself and decide what image I'd like to see. Then, I have to create that picture.

By changing how I think about a situation or event, I can change how I feel about it. Since thoughts and feelings lead to action, I am, in effect, changing how I respond. As a result, I'm much more likely to elicit the response I'd like to get from someone else.

Looking back I can see clearly the mistakes I made believing that cussing someone out was the way to get to them to change their behavior and do what I wanted them to do.

Here's the response I got one day when I was screaming through the phone at a man with whom I was angry for not behaving like I felt he should. "Ms. Swan," he asked, "why are you yelling at me like I'm a child?"

"Because," I said, "you're not listening to me. This is serious. Can't you see how upset I am?"

"I don't understand why you are so upset," he said, "but if you don't stop yelling at me I'm going to hang up the phone."

Why wasn't he responding like I wanted him to? I wondered. If he cared about me, the fact that I was so upset should be enough to inspire him to change his ways. If he didn't change, it meant he didn't care. Right? Wrong!

*If you don't like something change it; if you can't change it, change your attitude. ~ Maya Angelou*

Today, I can see how twisted that thinking was. People don't change just because we want them to. They only change when and if they want to. And no amount of yelling, cursing or crying is going to change that. It just makes the person doing the yelling, cursing and crying appear unhinged!

The only person I can control is me. If I don't like someone else's behavior there's nothing I can do to change him or her. I can accept it and respond accordingly. I can change how I see that person's behavior. Or, I can choose not to deal with that person. The choice and the responsibility to act are mine.

If we want to see changes in others, we have to change how we see them or we have to change ourselves.

# LESSON #6

*You are the only person you can change. If you want to see a difference in others, do something differently or think differently about what you see.*

## INNER WORK

### *BEING THE CHANGE YOU WANT TO SEE IN THE WORLD*

What is the one thing about yourself that, if changed, would have the most positive impact on your life?

Write a pledge to change it and begin the process to do so. Buy a book on the subject or consult a psychologist or other expert if necessary.

It's OK if you have to begin with baby steps. The important thing is to take that first step and to not beat yourself up along the way.

If you find that you're not making the progress you think you should, realize that you are doing the best you can and judging yourself only defeats the purpose.

# I Can Do Glad
# All By Myself

---

*~The single relationship that is truly central and crucial in a life is the relationship to the self. Of all the people you will know in a lifetime, you are the only one you will never lose. ~ Jo Coudert*

---

When Tom Cruise said, "You complete me," to Renee Zelwegger in that famous scene from Jerry Maguire – the one in which she responds, "You had me at hello" – the hearts of millions of women skipped a beat.

It's the happy ending they had been praying for in their own lives. Yet, for so many woman that dream stays just beyond our grasp.

So we flock to the theater for the steady diet of these fairy tales in which the princess finally finds her prince. It's irresistible - we hope one day to be that princess.

There's a central flaw to this attraction: we're buying into the premise that the answer to most women's problems is a man.

# Dancing to the Rhythm of My Soul

Consider Tyler Perry's films, *Madea's Family Reunion, Diary of a Mad Black Woman* and *I Can Do Bad All By Myself*.

First, let's make one thing clear: I am happy about Tyler's success. I've seen nearly all his movies and most of his plays. Most of his Madea films, however, are pretty much the same story with different faces. They, like so many flicks coming out of Hollywood, say romantic love, a male-female relationship, is a woman's ultimate desire. It is the final fulfillment and satisfaction of her life's purpose. But these films have a particular twist. In Tyler's films, the usual message – apart from the Christian themes - is that black women would have a better shot of finding happiness with a man if they "lowered" their standards. Add some bus drivers and factory workers to your list of potentials - along with the doctors and lawyers you hope for - and your chances of finding a good man increase exponentially.

It is, on the surface, a good premise. A man's character and what's in his heart should matter more than what is in his wallet. The problem with the films, though, is that the female characters all meet a man, see themselves through his eyes and then all becomes right with their world.

That's just not reality. The women in his films, have been abused physically, mentally and/or sexually. Yet, none of ever seek help or otherwise deal with these very serious issues (unless you count an exuberant sermon at a sanctified church).

The message is a woman unhappy with herself - one who hasn't taken the time to heal her mental and emotional wounds - will ultimately find happiness when she finds the right man.

Don't you believe it.

To attain a healthy relationship after a string of bad ones, a woman has to first figure out that she's the common denominator in all her failed relationships. The key is understanding why she keeps attracting "no-good" men.

In 2006, we got the interracial version of this theme with *Something New,* a film starring Sanaa Lathan who plays Kenya McQueen, an uptight sister with an attitude whose life is transformed when she allows herself to fall in love with a white man. And of course, there's a wedding at the end and all is well.

Again, I enjoyed the film. The premise – that black women should expand their options and not limit themselves to black men as potential companions, is certainly a relevant one that should be explored. However, like Jerry Maguire, the Tyler Perry films I mentioned, and most of the romantic movies coming out of Hollywood, they perpetuate the delusion that a woman who is unhappy with herself can find happiness simply by finding the right man.

## Dancing to the Rhythm of My Soul

Once you get past Kenya's good looks, the only thing appealing about her is her intellect. She isn't warm or friendly. In fact, she's downright prickly. She has no sense of humor. No sense of adventure. She surrounds herself in beige, which reflects her bland personality. And she wonders why she can't find a good man with whom to settle down?

Yes, it's romantic that Ralph helps Kenya find her other self - a woman who loves dogs, wears an array of colors and sports a natural hairdo instead of the weave that makes Corporate America more comfortable. That was sweet.

But seriously, how many men do you know who meet a woman who comes off like Cruella DeVille say to themselves, "She's the one?" Let's face it, Kenya was no walk in the park and not too many men would put up with her hostility in order to help her find herself.

In reality, we have to find ourselves by ourselves. No man can show us who we are. When we figure it out, though, we are far more likely to attract the kind of man we want.

While we are single, we should accept our singleness as the place we're supposed to be. To look at it any other way brings unnecessary misery.

Being single is not a disease. Nor is it a character defect. It's a box we check on a census form and a myriad of applications, but it says nothing about who we are as individuals.

Every time I meet a man who learns I'm single, the first question he asks is, "Why?"

I used to say it's because I haven't met the right man. Recently, I've decided to say, "It's the way I was born." It's the simple truth.

I often wonder what men expect to hear when they ask that question. "I'm a drama queen and no man wants me?" "I'm not the relationship type?" "I'm a recovering alcoholic?"

Society has decreed that women can't be happy by themselves and most of us have bought into the lie. There's nothing wrong with wanting to be part of a couple. It's human nature – and we are spiritual beings having a human experience – to want to share our lives with a partner.

There is something wrong, however, with the notion that being coupled is how we get to happy.

I know several coupled woman who will testify that marriage, shacking, and being booed up is hardly eternal bliss. Attaching ourselves to someone else is not the key to happiness. We are the relationship we've been looking for.

Happiness is not a tangible object in the possession of another – Mr. or Mrs. Right – which we get as a prize for finding him or her. It is an intangible experience, a choice that we make once we realize that the power to be happy has been ours all along. Happiness comes from within. As long as we look outside ourselves to find it, we will always be looking.

A miserable single woman will be a miserable girlfriend and/or a miserable wife. The only difference a relationship makes is she will have another person on whom to inflict her misery.

*The trouble is in our culture. We're all herded into the 'marriage/family' and somehow no matter how well our career is going, no matter how much social change you push for, no matter how much we're on our spiritual or religious path and no matter how well it's working, if we're not married (or at least in a committed relationship), somehow we're incomplete and that's a myth in our culture that is not true. ~ Peter McWilliams/ www.mcwilliams.com*

A happy single woman, one who is grateful, loving, aware and divine and who understands that she already is complete, will be a happy girlfriend and/or a happy wife. Being in a relationship allows her to share and grow that happiness with someone else. A spiritual partnership is a relationship between two authentically empowered people joined together to grow spiritually.

Women who look to men as a source of love will always be disappointed. No man, no matter how perfect we believe him to be, can love us the way we can love ourselves.

*You have so little faith in yourself because you are unwilling to accept the fact that perfect love is in you, and so you seek without for what you cannot find within. ~ A Course in Miracles*

As I stated earlier, the search for love is the search for self. What we think we need from a man – or a woman for our lesbian sisters – we can only get from ourselves. It's natural to yearn for romantic partnerships but it's important to understand that while such relationships can enrich our lives, they don't make our lives.

How many single, self-assured, successful, professional women do you know who are unhappy because they can't find a man? It's the one area of their life in which success remains elusive. At least if you define personal success as having a man. And many women do, even if they don't admit it.

Instead of embracing their singleness, they see it as a disease and a man, the right man, of course, is the cure.

I know because I've been there. I've shed many tears over the men I've had and The One I didn't. I have no problem getting a good job. A good man? Not so much. If my bed could talk it would tell you about the many lonely nights I spent wondering what in the world is wrong with me that scares off quality men. I believed, like so many women, that once I found Mr. Right all would be right in my world and I finally would be happy.

The truth is happiness comes when we find our authentic selves. The spiritual essence of our being that no one and nothing can destroy.

When we get in touch with the spirit that dwells within we can begin to heal our hurts, disappointments, anger, and pain. We can forgive. We can move on. We realize we are whole and complete, wanting nothing.

The woman who goes into a relationship for the experience of sharing love with another – not finding it – has a loving experience for as long as that relationship lasts.

If the relationship ends, she comes out of it just as whole as she went into it because she recognizes that her partner complements her. He doesn't complete her.

That doesn't mean she won't mourn the closing of that chapter of her life or miss her special someone. It does mean she's able to see the relationship as a learning experience and take the lesson – not the pain, anger, resentment and insecurity – into the next chapter.

Single people are single for a reason. Being single gives us time to find and work on ourselves. I needed to figure out why I kept attracting the same guy with a different face over and over again. The majority of the men who asked me out were liars and cheaters. Men who don't know what they want. I drew the men who, for a variety of reasons, were unavailable for a committed, monogamous relationship.

Was it because those men are all that's out there, as so many women claim? Or was there something about me that keeps this type of man gravitating toward me? After all, I am the common denominator here.

The bottom line is in order for me or any woman to be in a healthy love relationship with someone else, we must first prepare ourselves mentally and spiritually, no matter how long that takes, to be in a healthy love relationship with ourselves. And being single allows us to do that.

When we're ready, we will meet the right man or woman. If we want a relationship, and we've done the internal work to be ready for one, we can and will have one.

# Dancing to the Rhythm of My Soul

Don't get me wrong. I know the statistics.

Yale University researchers Natalie Nitsche and Hannah Brueckner found in an August, 2009 study that highly educated black women are twice as likely as highly educated white women to never have married by 45, and twice as likely to be divorced, widowed, or separated. Black women were least likely to be married to men with degrees. And the number of black men with degrees marrying outside their race - 14 percent - increased from 2000 to 2007.

The media, which loves negative stories, especially about black people, pounces on such statistics. In 2010, ABC's Nightline sponsored a packed town hall meeting titled *Why Can't a Successful Black Woman Find a Man?*

The panel featured comedian, author, and radio show host Steve Harvey, comedian Sherry Shepard of *The View*, actor and author Hill Harper, celebrity journalist Jacque Reid and author and blogger Jimi Israel.

Though I appreciate that the panel was mostly single black professionals sharing their stories, it would have been far more helpful to also have committed couples share how they met and how they maintain their relationships. A social scientist or psychologist would also have been a good idea. But the media, for the most part, is more interested in exploiting problems than helping to find solutions. Especially, when it comes to black folks.

The media has always been great at black pathology – telling us all the things that are wrong in our community. The sudden interest in the plight of the successful but single sista is no different.

And if the town hall wasn't enough to depress you, later that year, singer-songwriter Lyfe Jennings released *Statistics*, a single from his 2010 album, *I Still Believe.* According to Lyfe, 90 percent of all men fall into three categories. They are unstable, unfaithful or liars. We must wise up, he says, and choose our men from the remaining 10 percent.

I change the station every time I hear this song. The more we listen to the lyrics of tunes like *Statistics* and the thousands of other relationship gone bad songs the more we internalize the message that black women have a better chance of winning the lottery than finding a good man. And our beliefs become our reality.

Yes the numbers paint a pretty bleak picture for sisters looking for a husband, especially a black husband. But the numbers don't tell the whole story.

There are single women who meet great single men every day and enjoy great relationships. Some even walk down the aisle. If being coupled is what you want, you can be one of these women if you believe it's possible and stop settling for less than you want and deserve because you believe nothing else is possible.

The statistics don't have to be your reality.

Recently, I went on a jazz cruise where 99 percent of the attendees were black and 90 percent of them were in a relationship, most of them married. There was a young couple that looked to be in their late 20s or early 30s who were inseparable. They ran the karaoke session that took place on the ship nightly. One evening, he serenaded her with a Stevie Wonder song. It was beyond touching.

There was a middle aged couple celebrating their one year anniversary, illustrating that marriage isn't just for the young.

And an older couple that had been married more than 50 years who came out to hear the talent on open mike night.

Black love was alive but there were no television cameras to capture it. And even if there had been, chances are we'd never see the footage. Black couples in love, enjoying a seven-day cruise watching their favorite jazz musicians perform are not news.

Not long after that cruise, the federal government requested my presence in a West Palm Beach courtroom for jury duty. I was one of eight blacks in the potential jury pool. There were five brothers and three sisters, including myself.

We ranged in age from 32 to about 60. I was the only single one. The rest were married.

If we believe the hype, wouldn't the opposite have been true? The randomly selected group of Palm Beach County residents should have yielded a jury pool where all but one of the black folks was single because marriage, according to the media, is a middle class white phenomenon.

I cite these examples to illustrate that black women do marry. They do enjoy meaningful and fulfilling relationships with black men. Being a part of couple is not the impossibility we've been led to believe.

In the meantime, recognize that contrary to popular misconception, single is not a four letter word. It's not a disease or a character flaw to be cured or fixed. It is a great and often necessary place to be. Enjoy it!

If we can do bad all by ourselves, we certainly can do glad all by ourselves. Embrace the single life. Be the grateful, loving, aware and divine woman the Universe intended you to be. If a relationship is what you want, a grateful, loving, divine and aware man - or woman depending on your team – will come along when you're ready. And only when you're ready.

There are three reasons that I believe Barack Obama became the first African American president of the United States. 1) The country was ready for Mr. Obama and the change he claimed to represent. 2) He believed it was possible even when most people thought it was impossible. 3) He had prepared himself for the role.

We won't get what we want, whether it's a mate, a job or some long desired material possession until we are ready to receive it. We must believe our desires are possible and we must prepare ourselves to receive them.

There is a line in the song *Statistics* that I actually like. It is when Lyfe advises women to be the person they are looking for. Stacey, for instance, has a high school diploma she earned years after dropping out of school and wants a man with a college degree. Her credit score is poor, but she wants a man with great credit. She can't keep a job or an apartment, but wants a man with a good job and a nice house. It's highly unlikely the type of man she wants would want her.

The same is true for the obese woman who insists on a body builder or the loud and crass sister who insists on a man with class.

One of my favorite quotes from Mr. Obama's campaign is, "Change will not come if we wait for some other person or some other time. We are the ones we've been waiting for. We are the change that we seek."

His critics accused him of being arrogant. The fact is he was speaking truth to power – our power. The power to obtain what we want resides within us. We have to be the change we want to see in our lives.

Our external circumstances won't change until our internal circumstances do. So stop fretting over when you'll meet The One and do the internal work necessary to prepare yourself to become The One. Be the person you want to find.

# LESSON #7

*Single is not a four-letter word. It is the way we were born and it's the way we will leave here. The choice to be happily or unhappily single is ours.*

## INNER WORK

### *SINGLENESS ISN'T LONLINESS*

Create a photo slideshow or an album of pictures of yourself either solo or with friends doing the things you love.

At least three times a week, watch the slideshow or flip through the pictures to remind yourself how fabulous your life is right now, in this moment, as a single woman.

If you are married or partnered, you can do this, too, to remind yourself of the wonderful life you have as an individual outside of your romantic relationship.

# As a Woman Thinketh

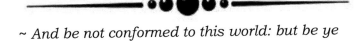

*~ And be not conformed to this world: but be ye transformed by the renewing of your mind ~ Romans 12:2.*

The Scripture above came to mind one evening as I was meditating, trying to find the peace that comes with silence and the absence of thought. Moments before I'd been in tears, upset by what I considered the thoughtless behavior of a loved one.

For some reason my mind got stuck on the word renewing. It didn't make sense! Renew means to make new again. How can something be new more than once? Then it hit me. It has to somehow become different.

But how, I wondered, do we make our minds different? By thinking different thoughts, of course!

Our minds are repositories of all the thoughts we've ever created, the memories we've stored, the pain we've endured and the joy we've experienced.

Every time something happens, every time someone says or does something, our mind tells us how to interpret it; how to react. It does this by drawing upon what's already there. The process is so automatic we don't even realize it is taking place.

Most of us are on automatic pilot, acting and reacting without even considering the reason for our behavior or feelings. If we don't want to be part of this pattern, we must change what's stored in our minds. If not, we will continue to interpret and react to situations and events the same way over and over again. To expect something different would be like waiting for a computer to load a program that doesn't exist!

We have to upgrade our RAM – random access memory – and install new software.

As I lay on my couch, no longer meditating but processing this information as it flooded my mind, I realized why the Scripture had come to me. I wanted to be able to react differently than I had to the behavior that had so bothered me. I didn't want to be in tears every time someone didn't behave or respond in the manner that I wanted. I had chosen to meditate because I knew that I needed to focus my attention on me instead of the other person to feel better. I needed to take back my emotions from his control and put them into mine.

What's more powerful, though, is never giving up that control in the first place. And that's the transformation that results when we renew our minds. We can choose to think and feel differently about people, places, things, situations and events. Those different thoughts lead to different actions and different responses.

By changing our minds we change our perception of the people in our lives and our interpretations of their behavior. We recognize that the only power they have is the power we give them. That power comes from our thoughts - how we choose to think.

In researching the idea that thoughts have power and we alone control those thoughts, I came across a book written more than 100 years ago by James Allen called *As a Man Thinketh.*

"As a being of Power, Intelligence, and Love, and the lord of his own thoughts, man holds the key to every situation, and contains within himself that transforming and regenerative agency by which he may make himself what he wills," writes Allen. "Just as a gardener cultivates his plot, keeping it free from weeds, and growing the flowers and fruits which he requires, so may a man tend the garden of his mind, weeding out all the wrong, useless, and impure thoughts, and cultivating toward perfection the flowers and fruits of right, useful, and pure thoughts.

"By pursuing this process, a man sooner or later discovers that he is the master gardener of his soul, the director of his life. He also reveals, within himself, the laws of thought, and understands with ever-increasing accuracy, how the thought forces and mind elements operate in the shaping of his character, circumstances, and destiny."

Wow! How empowering is it to know that we are in control? That there is no mysterious force out there exerting its power over our lives?

It's not only empowering; it's scary.

Scary because if we accept that we have total responsibility for our lives, it means we can no longer blame anyone else. That is why so many of us prefer to conform to the ways of this world rather than transform.

But transform we must if we hope to have the harmonious and love-filled life experiences we desire.

Our thoughts have the power to create. Thoughts precede action. Before we say something or do something, we think it first. So to bring about change in our lives, we must change the way we think. That in turn changes how we speak and what we do.

If you doubt the power of thoughts, think about the last time someone hurt your feelings. Or the last time you used words as a weapon to hurt someone else. Now, try to recall a time when words healed a hurt, either yours or someone else's.

Thoughts are composed of words. They can be spoken or unspoken, but either way they have great power. As our thoughts go, our lives go. Think of thoughts as software. The operating system of the mind, which controls all that we say and do, and therefore all that we experience.

The day after I purchased a new car, a man in a mini-van rear ended me, smashing my bumper and injuring my back. Moments after the accident, I realized that I had willed it to occur. Not purposefully, of course, but with my thoughts.

For some reason, that whole day I had been worried about my new car getting damaged and I kept hoping that it wouldn't happen. The thoughts became so powerful; I began to get anxious. Later that night, the accident occurred.

Coincidence? Many would probably say so. I have no doubt, though, that had I been thinking positive thoughts – being grateful for the new car instead of fearful of losing it – the accident never would have happened!

I was listening to Dr. Robin Smith promote her book, *Lies at the Altar: The Truth About Great Marriages,* on the radio one morning when someone asked her whether black women were angry. She responded that yes, indeed, they were and one reason for their miserable relationships was that we attract what we are. I hadn't yet begun my spiritual transformation so at the time; I took this statement personally. First, I was not angry. Second, what the hell did she mean we attract what we are? I'm not a triflin' liar and cheater like so many of the men I seemed to attract! How dare she!

I came to realize it's not that we attract what we are, but what we believe. If I believe that all men are dogs, then why would a good man want to be with me? Our beliefs are nothing more than what we think. And those thoughts determine our experiences.

Years before my mother's stroke, she talked often about having one. She'd have coughing fits and each time, she'd swear she was having a stroke or dying. She was the epitome of a drama queen. Once she was standing at the stove cooking when one of her coughing attacks hit and she started screaming. My sister and I raced into the kitchen where she pulled a Fred Sanford - the move where he puts one hand across his chest and raises the other hand to the sky as he shouts to the heavens and alerts his deceased wife Elizabeth that he's on his way to join her.

"Don't cry for me," my mother said in her most dramatic fashion. "I've lived a good life."

My sister, a drama queen like my mother, began to scream hysterically, thinking our mother was on her way to join Elizabeth, too! I told her to calm down as I prepared for another long wait in the emergency room for the doctors to tell us for the umpteenth time that our mother was fine.

Later, I told my mother that she had spoken her stroke into existence with all her negative thinking and shouts of, "I'm having a stroke. Take me to the hospital!" She says that she always had a feeling that she would suffer a catastrophic illness and often prayed that God would allow her to live long enough to see her first grandchild.

Both happened. Her thoughts of a catastrophic illness became a consuming fear and ultimately a reality. And that first grandchild was my son who now has a son of his own. My mother has lived long enough to see 19 grandchildren and five great-grandchildren.

She is living proof that our thoughts have power. So is Andrea.

Andrea is a 40-year-old, professional, single sister who's never been married and has no children. She's nice looking, has a great career, makes good money, owns a gorgeous home and has a host of friends, but yearns for a husband and kids. She's pretty bleak, though, about her prospects. Her dating life has consisted of a series of duds, men with self-esteem issues who are unemployed or underemployed and want to do nothing but lay up in her house. Then there are the amnesiacs who conveniently forget the trips they made to the altar.

"I believe there are good men out there," Andrea says. "On Jupiter!"

Well, with thinking like that, Jupiter will be the only place she finds one.

Just as Carmen may never attract the type of man she really wants because she doesn't believe she's worthy of him. She says she'd never consider dating a doctor. A plumber or an electrician? No problem. Not that there's anything wrong a plumber or electrician, but why does not feel qualified to date a doctor?

Divorced with a teenage son, she's not necessarily looking for the white picket fence. She would like a monogamous relationship with a man on her level financially and intellectually. She's an educated professional with a great job, and her own home. She's also pretty, keeps in shape, and has great friends. Carmen keeps abreast of current events and is more than capable of holding her own in a conversation with a doctor, a lawyer or any other reasonably intelligent sentient being. Still, she doesn't think she's worthy of a doctor. That might explain why men who are her financial, intellectual and emotional equal seldom cross her path. And those who do are rarely looking for a relationship. Her thoughts, which translate into her beliefs, are creating her reality. If we believe that we are unworthy of something or someone then that something or someone is not likely to enter our space. And if they do, we won't be able to enjoy the experience.

Do you laugh at the notion that thinking positive can bring about significant change in our lives? You're ignoring the scientific evidence. Studies show that positive thinking improves our health. High stress has been proven to be detrimental to our health.

One researcher studied healthy newlywed couples to see how their stress levels changed when they talked about their marriage. She measured their levels of the stress hormone cortisol that increases with negative emotions.

In the study, the cortisol level spiked when the spouses used negative words and dropped when they used positive words.

My friend Tina is living proof of the power of positive thinking. Her mother died of breast cancer so she's been vigilant about getting mammograms and physicals. Turns out she, too, would get the disease. Not once, but three times.

Ironically, the third time doctors discovered cancer it was after she'd had a mastectomy, hoping to prevent it from recurring. Trying to be proactive, she decided to lose the offending breast and get a prosthetic one. After the mastectomy doctors learned that the cancer had returned.

Devastation, however, wasn't an option for Tina. She knows how much her mental health affects her physical health. She prayed daily and listened to her favorite gospel tunes to keep her spirits up and her thoughts positive. She had made up her mind that the cancer wasn't going to win.

Today, Tina, who is 42, never married and childless, is cancer free. Chemotherapy and the cancer drugs she has to take for the next several years may make having biological children difficult, but she hasn't given up hope. And I've never once heard her complain. She happily dates and lives life one day at a time, grateful for each sunrise. She is a positive thinker enjoying a positive life.

Positive thinking doesn't mean ignoring the dark events that occur in our lives. It means that we see these events in a more positive light and handle them in a positive way. It means we don't wallow in the darkness, but seek the lesson. Remember positive circumstances do not result from negative thoughts.

Think positive for a healthy body, a healthy mind and a positive life.

# LESSON #8

*Thoughts have the power to create or destroy. Think positively to create the great life you want and deserve.*

## INNER WORK

### *THINKING POSITIVELY*

Take time out from your day to watch your thoughts. Close your eyes and sit in a quiet place. Don't try to control your thoughts. Just let them come.

As you do this, imagine your hands on a giant DELETE button. When the negative thoughts enter your mind, imagine yourself pressing the button and physically deleting them.

When positive thoughts enter, welcome them with a smile. Let them linger. Focus your attention on them. Allow yourself to feel their impact.

Also, meditating on the list you made of things for which you're grateful will help you maintain positive thoughts and positive energy.

# The Mother Load

---●•◉•●---

*~ There is no such thing as guilt, you cannot go to the store and buy a pound or bag of guilt. It is a man-made ego minded emotion that is detrimental to humans living to their full potential. ~ Jenn Prothero*

---●•◉•●---

In American culture, women value themselves based on their relationships. This is especially true for black women who have always been known for the ferocity with which we love and protect our families. That reputation is holding, despite movies like *Precious* and the media's insistent portrayal of us as crack whores and welfare queens who use our children like poker chips.

For many of us who are mothers, our self-image is intrinsically tied to our children. They are, after all, a part of us. We created them. We love them beyond all others. And we are, we believe, responsible for how they turn out.

What happens, though, when our children don't turn out the way we hoped? When they behave in ways that go against everything we taught them?

Many of us play the blame game. We torture ourselves with guilt, wondering how we could have done things differently. We live a life filled with regrets.

Society has conditioned us to believe that guilt and regrets are the byproduct of parenting. There isn't a parent on earth who doesn't wish they could have done something differently. Guilt and regret are universal emotions.

This is true despite the fact that they are useless. Guilt and regret serve no good purpose. They are beneficial tools to those who would manipulate or try to control us. But what have regrets done for you lately?

Regardless of how our children turn out, our job is to love them without judgment, do our best to guide them, and accept that they are where they are supposed to be.

I learned this the hard way.

My children have always been my world. In my mind's eye I can still see my oldest son, who is now 28, as a baby. I would read to him every night before bed and when I tucked him in I'd say, "I love you more than anything in the whole wide world."

Whenever I asked him, "How much do I love you?" He'd respond, "More than anything in the whole wide world."

That love, however, would not protect him from himself. Nor would it protect my second son from himself, either.

My children have had every advantage. They had my love. My time. My involvement in their lives. They had the middle class lifestyle my income could provide.

They lacked nothing they needed and little of what they wanted. Still, my boys couldn't resist the lure of the streets or the influence of young men who attracted trouble like a magnet. Nothing I did or said could protect them. Their peers had their ears and their loyalty.

It's hard to come to terms with the fact that no matter how well we believe we do our jobs as parents, our children may still make bad choices. Still walk a path that we'd go through fire to help them avoid.

I had to come to terms with this fact.

I was on a Delaware highway headed to a meeting for work when my ringing cell phone pulled my attention away from what was playing on the radio. "Are you sitting down?" my sister asked.

"I'm driving. I guess that counts as sitting down."

"Pull over."

"Why?"

"You don't need to be on the road."

My heart began to race as I steered my Honda Civic into the break down lane.

"Before I tell you what happened," my sister said, "I want you to know that Seneca's alright."

She then recounted the story of how my eldest child had been the victim of a home invasion. Thugs had kicked in the door of the house he shared with two roommates and pistol whipped him before attacking the others. For a while, he played possum, pretending to be unconscious from his injuries, before jetting out the front door. His attackers followed, shooting at his back as he made his way down the street to a convenience store.

Thankfully, the bullets missed.

I made it to my meeting, but couldn't focus. Even knowing that my son was alright couldn't keep my mind away from what could have been. Unable to think of anything except Seneca, I left in the middle of the meeting. A few days later while working out alone at the gym; the reality that I'd nearly lost my son overwhelmed me. I couldn't escape the images of him running barefoot for his life, dodging a hail of bullets as rain pelted down on his fear stricken body. The weights I'd been lifting dropped to the floor. My body followed. I fell into the fetal position and wailed.

Dancing to the Rhythm of My Soul

That, unfortunately, would not be Seneca's only near death experience. The following year, I was riding along another highway when I got another call.

"Ma, did you hear?" asked my daughter.

"Hear what?"

"Sinny got shot!"

Air ceased to fill my lungs. My heart pounded so hard I thought it would burst from my chest. Images of Seneca lying on an operating table, gasping for air, flickered through my mind like previews to a movie.

My daughter had no other information. She couldn't tell me the extent of Seneca's wounds or his condition.

I was about 20 minutes away from the hospital where Seneca had been taken. It was the longest 20 minutes of my life.

When I arrived, more than a dozen of Seneca's cousins and friends were lined up outside the emergency room looking as somber as I felt. I couldn't even utter a hello. After insisting that the security guards let me behind the locked metal doors to the treatment area, I learned that he had been lucky enough to suffer only a flesh would. The bullet went straight through his thigh. He was going to be OK.

But for how long? Despite my best efforts, Seneca had chosen to run in the company of people who carried guns to settle their arguments.

It wouldn't be long before his younger brother would follow the same path. Only Stephon wasn't as lucky as Seneca. He always got caught.

My second son has celebrated every birthday since 18 in a county jail. He's 24. He ran away at 17 because I insisted that he get an education and a job and wear pants that couldn't fit the both of us. But he didn't want to do things my way. He'd gotten a taste of the easy life.

When Hurricane Wilma hit Florida in 2005, they predicted we'd be without power for at least two weeks. No power meant we'd be without a refrigerator, stove, lights, TV, radio and the Internet. And no school!

I sent Stephon and my daughter to Massachusetts to ride out Wilma's after effects at my sister's. But my sister barely saw Stephon. He went missing, hanging with his cousins and their friends in the 'hood. These young men, who had no parents looking out for them, were hustling on street corners and playing house with girls whose babies qualified them for welfare and Section 8 housing subsidies. Stephon, who for some reason I'll never understand had always idolized the ghetto life glorified in rap music, wanted to live like his cousins.

Soon after he returned to Florida, he begged me to let him move back to Springfield. I knew nothing good awaited him there. I insisted that until he turned 18, he would live under my roof and under my rules. Little did I know that a man he met during his brief visit had bought him a train ticket to Springfield where he had a "job" lined up for Stephon. I knew that so-called job could be nothing other than a street corner pharmaceutical salesman.

One evening, after we argued for the umpteenth time over his moving to Springfield, he left and never came back. I reported him as a runaway, but police don't make 17-year-old black boys a high priority.

Stephon drew the interest of the police soon enough. He moved in with a 20-year-old mother of four. He fancied himself the man of her house, an apartment on a trash strewn block in the heart of a poverty stricken neighborhood. He made friends with the neighborhood thugs and began living a hustler's life.

He was only in Springfield a few months when police caught him selling drugs. A couple of months later, they'd catch him again. He got probation both times. I resigned myself to the fact that he was fully cooked and he was living the life that he wanted. He knew there was a room for him in my home. There was, however, nothing I could say or do to force him to take advantage of it.

Stephon would eventually get five years in jail followed by eight years of probation for participating in a fight that wasn't even his.

One of his so-called friends was getting a beat down when he decided to knock on Stephon's door for back up. Always the follower, Stephon joined him outside. The next thing he knew, this friend threw him a gun and told him to shoot. Stephon did, aiming in no particular direction as he fled the scene in fear. One of the bullets went through a window in a nearby apartment, ricocheting off the wall and hit a boy who was visiting relatives.

When he first told me the details, I hung up on Stephon and began praying for the little boy and his family. My son was in trouble – again – and I ached for him, but my heart also was aching for the mother of that little boy.

Unfortunately, I knew how she felt and I desperately wanted her son to be alive. Physically, he was. His wound was minor. Sadly, even though he'd gotten it through no action on his part, the boy thought the bullet wound gave him street cred. No sooner than the hospital discharged him, he was running around the neighborhood bragging about getting shot. Now I pray that he doesn't follow the same path as my son.

I have spent more nights than I can count crying over my sons and wondering where I went wrong. I didn't just teach them the value of hard work, a good education, strength of character, and family loyalty, I showed them.

The only thing I couldn't give them was a father. Theirs had abandoned them. The courts can force a man to pay child support, but they can't force him to parent his child.

Still, there are plenty of men who grow up without fathers and don't choose the path of least resistance.

My mother, who didn't go to college, single-handedly raised five children – three of them sons – and all five have college degrees, good jobs and are successful by society's standards. Why have my children chosen such different paths?

I don't have the answer. What I do have, though, is peace of mind.

After my brother and I talked Stephon into turning himself in for the shooting, I flew to Springfield to see him. Later that evening, I was at my sister's and couldn't stop crying because the whole family was there, except him. There was a hole in my heart nothing could fill.

When he called from jail that night, I asked Stephon if there was anything I could have done differently to keep him from the choices he'd made.

"Ma, I know this is not the life you wanted me to have," he said. "There's nothing you could've done different. I made the decisions that put me here."

Ain't that the truth.

Those words didn't just free me from the guilt I had been feeling – which I know now that I had no reason to feel – they let me know that Stephon was finally taking responsibility for his own actions, something that until that point he had failed to do.

No matter how great a job we do raising our children, ultimately their lives are in their hands. There comes a point in all of our lives when we can no longer blame our parents for the choices we make. When each of us has to take responsibility for the life that we ourselves create. Our children must get to that point, too. Some will do it sooner than others. Some may never do it at all.

We have to face that fact that our daughters will ultimately lose their virginity, many much sooner than we would've wanted. Our sons will take someone's virginity, many much sooner than we would've wanted. They will choose careers with which we may not agree. They will choose partners we may not like. And they will make mistakes – lots of mistakes. We can only hope they will be mistakes from which they can learn and recover.

Our children are a part of us, but they are not us. They each have their own personalities and their own souls. They will have to figure out how to get in touch with their spirits just as we have to figure out how to get in touch with ours. They will have their own lessons to learn just as we do. We can guide them to the best of our ability, but we cannot live their lives.

One evening while folding laundry and listening to the radio, the song, *If I Could* by Regina Belle began to play. I'd heard the tune dozens of times, but this was the first time I really listened to the lyrics.

*If I could/I would try to shield your innocence from time/But the part of life I gave you isn't mine/I'll watch you grow, so I can let you go/If I could/I would help you make it through the hungry years/But I know that I can never cry your tears, babe /But I would/If I could*

The words spoke my heart and I began to cry. How many of us would cry our children's tears and suffer their pain if we could? There was a time when I would think of Stephon and wish I could trade places with him. Do his time. I would worry over whether he was warm enough. Whether they were feeding him enough. I would worry about his mental health. He tends to stress over everything.

As mothers, we want to take away all of our children's hurts. We don't want them to suffer for a single second. But as I lay across my bed that evening beside my unfolded laundry, trying to exhale the anxiety that had stopped by for a visit, I remembered that Stephon was where he was supposed to be. If I were able to do his time, he wouldn't get the lesson that his experience in jail is supposed to teach.

I knew that for the most part he was safe. Safer than he'd been on the streets. He's seen men twice his age come and go more than once in the few years he's been locked up. Men who still haven't gotten the lesson. Who may not get the lesson in this lifetime.

*I don't believe in guilt. I believe in living on impulse as long as you never intentionally hurt another person, and don't judge people in your life. I think you should live completely free. ~ Angelina Jolie*

Stephon literally has grown up in jail.

I'd like to believe that he will be a wiser young man now that he's free than he was when he went in. I've tried to teach him some of the lessons I've learned on my journey, such as the need to forgive his father for abandoning him. So many of his mistakes, after all, were the result of that deep-seated anger he feels toward his father.

# Dancing to the Rhythm of My Soul

Like most children of abandonment, he simply cannot comprehend his father's lack of involvement in his life. Stephon has been trying to make him pay for that abandonment ever since. When his dad did make the occasional effort, Stephon rebuffed him. He even refused his father's visits to the jail.

Whenever I bring up the topic of forgiveness, Stephon tells me that his dad is the adult and that as the parent he should ask for Stephon's forgiveness. I tell him that his dad is unaware and that based on his level of spiritual maturity he may never do what Stephon expects. After all, the reason his relationship with his father is so strained is because the man failed to live up to his expectations.

I tell him that it's not about his dad, it's about him. If Stephon is to be free of the pain that his animus towards his father has caused, he must free himself through forgiveness.

For now though, Stephon can only focus on his physical, not his mental freedom. Life hasn't been easy for him since he got out. He's a black man with a felony record. A gun charge at that. But I tell him to take responsibility for his actions and to think positively. I tell him to believe that everything will be all right and that it will be.

I believe it.

I don't cry myself to sleep at night anymore. I don't live with guilt or regret. Not just about my children, but about anything. I have done the best that I can at my level of awareness and so have you.

Though we are our children's teachers, they also are ours. We learn a great many lessons from them about who we are and about the world.

Through my children I have learned unconditional love and to live life guilt free and without regrets.

The reality is we feel guilty when we believe we have failed to live up to expectations - those that others have of us, including society at large, and those we have of ourselves.

Even if we decide that those expectations are worthwhile, the fact that we didn't live up to them is because we were unable to do so based on who we were at that time. The woman you are today might make different choices, but the woman you were then made the choices she was capable of then.

Today, both Seneca and Stephon would almost surely make different choices than they did as teenagers. But they are not the men today that they were then. The choices they made then are what made them the men they are today.

Seneca is now the father of a son. He already is a different father to his son than his father was to him. The love he feels for his little boy is apparent to anyone who sees him. He wants to give his son a good life and he knows that means he must be around. I believe he will make the choices necessary.

Still, I will love him, his brother and his sister unconditionally and without judgment no matter their choices. And I will teach them to regret and feel guilty for nothing. Though we can and should try to make amends for that which we believe we did wrong in the past, there's certainly nothing we can do to change the past. We can only learn from it and do better as we know better.

# LESSON #9

*Guilt serves no purpose.*
*Don't give it one in your life.*

## INNER WORK
## DISPENSING WITH GUILT

Make a list of the people you have offended and toward whom you feel guilty. Call or write them to apologize and seek their forgiveness. It doesn't matter whether or not they forgive you. What's important is that you make the effort. Once you do, there is no reason for you to feel guilty anymore. You did the best you could at your level of awareness and now you have done your best to make amends.

For those guilty feelings that remain – regrets for things you wish you'd done differently or choices you wish you could make again – make a list of those that bother you the most. Close your eyes and meditate on that list, breathing in deeply and allowing yourself to feel the guilt for as long as you can stand it. Now exhale. Imagine all that guilt being released with your breath and disappearing into the air. It's now invisible. You can no longer grab and hold onto it. It is no longer real. Let it go.

Now take your list and destroy it. Burn it or shred it. Make it, too, disappear.

# Playing the Victim

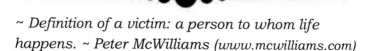

*~ Definition of a victim: a person to whom life happens. ~ Peter McWilliams (www.mcwilliams.com)*

When the executive director of an agency that helps battered women asked me to be the keynote speaker at a fundraising event, I had no idea what to talk about.

I'd been hit by a man – more than one actually - but I didn't consider myself an abused woman because the men who hit me learned quickly not to do so again.

So I asked the director if there was a particular message she was hoping to hear from me. She said she wanted me to encourage the women to stop living their lives as victims. Her clients, she said, were wallowing in self-pity, using the fact that they had been battered as an excuse for not moving forward with their lives. And in many cases, their children also were suffering because the mothers used their victim status as an excuse for ineffective parenting.

In essence, these women had given power over their lives to the men who had battered them. Despite the fact that the men were clearly unprepared for the job, they had given them the title of CEO, chief executive overseer of their fate.

That's what we do when we play the victim. We abdicate our authority over ourselves and put it in someone else's hands.

It doesn't take a man going upside our heads to make us choose the victim role. It could be anything. A run of bad luck, a series of no-good men, a dysfunctional childhood, or just life circumstances can lead us to assume the position. And why not? Playing the victim is the easy way out. It lets us off the hook. We don't have to be responsible for our choices and decisions if we can blame them on anything or anyone but ourselves. Playing the victim allows us to be right and others wrong. They are the villains for treating us the way they do and we are the good but helpless damsels in distress.

The problem with this thinking is that it gets us absolutely nowhere. While we sit around feeling sorry for ourselves, doing nothing for ourselves, life continues to go on and we miss out on all the good it has to offer.

We are only victims if we choose to be. It's only when we stop acting as though we are powerless and accept responsibility for the life we created that we obtain the power to change it for the better. A woman who won't leave a man who abuses her body and her mind chooses to give him control over her life. Abused women have plenty of reasons for staying: financial stability, emotional attachment and fear, to name a few. Regardless of the reason, though, the result is the same. Their lives are not their own.

The same is true for those of us who stay in any kind of relationship or situation - including a job - where we feel victimized or less than fulfilled. Whether we stay because we are afraid to be alone, afraid to lose the security of a full time job with benefits, or just simply afraid of change, fear controls our lives.

When we choose to be victors instead of victims, we choose freedom. We become the masters of our destiny. It's up to us to make change happen if we want it. That means realizing that we are the authors, directors and producers of our lives. Everything we see on the screen begins and ends with us.

I lived as a victim for many years, blaming my circumstances on bad luck, bad men and bad timing. One day, while visiting my cousin in Chicago, I was complaining about my son Stephon's "deadbeat" father when my cousin said, "You picked him."

"What's that supposed to mean?" I asked, offended that I was being blamed for this man's behavior.

"You picked him," he repeated.

He explained that he was tired of hearing women complain about the no-good men in their lives as though they bore no responsibility for their situation. I didn't see it at the time, but later I realized he was right.

My son's dad may have been a sorry father, but what was it about me that had attracted him into my life? And why did I put up with his behavior way longer than I should have?

I don't for one minute regret having my son, but the reality is I should have taken more time to get to know his father and figure out what kind of father he was going to be.

If I had, I would've realized that he was not good father material. His mother had abandoned him and handed him off to his father. His father then handed him off to an aunt who raised him.

He was so emotionally handicapped that when his mother became gravely ill, he told me that he didn't know how to feel. The woman hadn't been a mother to him. "Am I supposed to cry? Am I supposed to feel bad," he asked. Was it normal to not feel sad?

We show love to others the way others show love to us. We support and care for others the way others support and care for us. If no one has

133

ever shown us how to express love, care or support, we won't know how to do it...unless we choose to learn. Choose to break the cycle.

Stephon's father chose to continue the cycle. I chose him without the full understanding of how his early experiences had shaped him. The signs that he would not be an involved and loving parent were there, if I had been paying attention.

Though I had been asleep at the wheel in my relationship, Tremaine was wide awake. She knew exactly what kind of man the father of her children was when she married him. Wayman had serious anger management issues, a violent temper and he often beat her.

One day while I was visiting, Wayman threw Tremaine down, took her head and started slamming it against the hard wood floor of their apartment. I tried to pull him off her, but he pushed me into the wall. I grabbed her son, a toddler at the time, and ran to a neighbor's and called the police.

The officers just took Wayman for a walk and told him to calm down. When I asked why they didn't arrest him when I was willing to give a statement, one of the officers responded that too often the victim bails out her abuser and he's home in time for dinner. So making an arrest would be, he said, a waste of everyone's time.

Turns out he was right.

# Dancing to the Rhythm of My Soul

To my surprise, Tremaine agreed to be Wayman's wife not long after that brutal incident. If marriage was going to change Wayman at all, I warned her, it would only change him for the worse. Still, she took that walk down the aisle. Not surprisingly, years later, after one fight too many – Tremaine always fought back – they divorced. Alas, she picked him.

I'm not suggesting that Tremaine is responsible for Wayman's abuse. He alone is responsible for his behavior. Tremaine is, however, responsible for the choice to be in relationship with him. For being his wife. For knowingly subjecting herself to his violent ways.

The people in our lives are there because we allow them to be. Whether we choose them or let them choose us, we are a willing participant in the process. Once we accept that we are responsible for the choices that have placed us where we are, we are free and empowered to make different and better choices. We can take constructive action to move on with our lives.

Even victims of the most heinous crimes have found a way to move past what happened to them. You can, too.

Victor Frankl, an internationally renowned psychotherapist and author, was a Holocaust survivor who believed that there's nothing a human being can't overcome as long as we understand that our life has meaning. Frankl, who lived in four German concentration camps, including Auschwitz, over a period of five years, said many survivors endured because they refused to give in to feelings of victimization.

The Nazis took their physical freedom, their worldly possessions, and in many cases, slaughtered their families. They couldn't, however, take away their spirit or their ability to choose their thoughts and feelings.

"We must never forget that we may also find meaning in life even when confronted with a hopeless situation, when facing a fate that cannot be changed," Frankl wrote in his bestselling book, *Man's Search for Meaning.* "For what then matters is to bear witness to the uniquely human potential at its best, which is to transform a personal tragedy into a triumph, to turn one's predicament into a human achievement."

Like Victor Frankl, Patty was a victim of circumstances beyond her control. She was jogging in a park when a man appeared from nowhere and raped her. The police caught him and he's been in prison for more than two decades. The parole board has denied him several times. Every time he's up for consideration, though, Patty becomes terrified. She fears he will come after her again and she repeatedly relives the rape in her mind.

She panics and contemplates moving out of state. She doesn't want to. Her family is there.

Her husband's family is there. It's the only home her two young boys have ever known. But what if her rapist finds her there?

Patty's therapist explained to her that as long as she continues to fear her attacker, she gives him power over her. She cannot let the fear paralyze her to the point that she stops enjoying her life. She has to take back control. She has to accept that her rapist will return to society one day and there's nothing she can do about it. She cannot let that consume her.

In other words, she has to stop being his victim. He's taken far too much from her already.

Patty is not responsible for what happened to her. Her fear is something we can all understand. And she illustrates how much the events of the past can strangle us in the present, if we let them. Whenever we host pity parties, we are playing the victim. Allowing ourselves to be prisoners of the past.

Victors live in the present. They are fearless. They don't let life happen to them. They take life by the reins. No matter what.

Patty has chosen to attack her fear. To take back from her rapist the power over her life that he stole. "You can't," she said, "let someone else's inexcusable actions define what you do with your life."

She is a victim turned victor.

If Patty can do it, I know you can.

# LESSON #10

*You can only be a victim if you allow yourself to be. Choose to overcome.*

## INNER WORK

### *TAKING BACK YOUR POWER*

Find a quiet space where you can be alone without interruption. Take several deep breaths. As you inhale, slowly allow your body to relax and empty your mind of thoughts.

Imagine you are in a place where you feel completely safe, at peace and happy. Stay with that image for as long as it takes for the good feelings that place evokes to arise. Mentally bathe in those feelings and allow them to warm you.

Repeat the following affirmation:

I am stronger than any weapon used against me. I am successful. I am a winner.

Do this as often as it takes for you to believe this. You will know that you believe when your actions begin to reflect these words.

# Judge Not,
# Lest Ye Be Judged

*~ Everything that irritates us about others can lead us to an understanding of ourselves. ~ Carl Jung*

If your name isn't Judge Judy, Judge Joe Brown, Judge Mathis or Judge Hatchett, it's not your job to decide whether other people are right, wrong, good or bad.

Judging – ourselves and other people – is one of the major impediments to our growth into mature, spiritual beings. Yet, it is as natural to most of us as breathing. We judge everything and everyone that comes into our presence.

What we don't understand, however, is that every time we pass judgment on someone or something, we also are passing judgment on ourselves. That's because what we choose to judge in others is what we don't like about ourselves. That's why we notice it in the first place.

Take for example, an incident that occurred on a Florida highway while I was riding with David. The car in front of us was practically crawling and David was having a fit, yelling at the driver as though the man actually could hear him. I could almost see his blood pressure rising. I put my hand on his arm and began to caress it, asking him in my most soothing voice to calm down. He snatched his arm away. "Don't," he shouted, "patronize me!"

Wow. Is it that serious? I thought. Seconds later, though, a smile crept across my face as I realized I was watching myself. Only months prior, that had been me. Prone to road rage and cussing out other drivers as though they had bionic hearing. If the situation had been reversed and David had been the one trying to calm me down, I would've reacted in the exact same way he had - with my ego.

David and I are mirror images of each other. So, instead of getting offended at his reaction to my efforts to soothe him, I decided to just let him be. I knew that when my ego was in control there was little anyone else could say to get me to see things other than the way my ego wanted to see them. The ego thrives off anger and righteous indignation. If I tried to convince David that he needed to behave differently, his ego would have snapped at me louder. The best thing for me to do was be a silent observer.

Too often, though, we judge others harshly for behavior we are guilty of ourselves. Anytime someone talks with fervor about how much they detest a certain behavior in others, I usually conclude that it's a behavior with which they are struggling.

The promiscuous sister who is quick to call someone a slut. The aggressive driver who gets outraged at tailgaters. The spendthrift who can't stand cheapskates.

When we spend so much of our time judging others, there's little left to work on ourselves. But as long as there are others doing less than, being less than us, we can justify doing less than and being less than.

I see a heavy set woman walking down the street and immediately, I say to myself, "Damn! I would never let myself get that big!" In other words, I know I need to get my butt to the gym to get off these extra pounds I have no business carrying but hell, at least I ain't as bad as her. Now, I can justify skipping the gym for yet another week!

We all are guilty of judging. What we rarely do is take the time to ask ourselves what benefit judging provides us. Absolutely none!

Robin would beg to differ. She believed that judging allowed her to make clear choices about

how she did and didn't want to live her life.
Parent her children. Treat her husband. So when
I shared with her stories about other people in my
life she would instantly judge them, saying such
things as, "I would never do that."

Whenever I mentioned that I was practicing
non-judgment, she'd say that she needed to judge
so she'd know how not to behave. Do we really
need to see and pass judgment on a crack addict
to know that crack is whack? It really doesn't
take labeling others as good or bad, right or
wrong, to determine the best course of action for
our lives.

"You do not need judgment to organize your
life," says *A Course In Miracles*, "and you certainly
do not need it to organize yourself."

As often as I can remember, I repeat this
prayer from the Course, "Today I shall judge
nothing that occurs." I say it in my mind
whenever I see something or someone that
provokes me to judge. Practicing non-judgment
helps to keep us in the moment, which is the only
place to find peace.

"The choice to judge rather than to know is
the cause of the loss of peace," says the Course.
"Judgment is the process on which perception
but not knowledge rests. Judgments always
involve rejection. It never emphasizes only the
positive aspects of what is judged, whether in you
or in others. You have no idea of the tremendous

release and deep peace that comes from meeting yourself and your brothers totally without judgment."

When I'm judging others – or judging myself – I'm creating unnecessary mental noise. There are enough thought wars taking place in my mind without me having to worry about why the woman in the Walmart checkout line decided to paint each of her toe nails a different color - yellow, green, orange, red and blue. I see it, tell myself that I will judge nothing that occurs and chalk it up to self-expression and none of my business. That way, I can focus on me and quieting the other thoughts competing for my attention and trying to remove me from the present moment.

*Knowing your own darkness is the best method for dealing with the darknesses of other people. ~ Carl Jung*

I won't, however, pretend that it's easy. Judging is what we do. Our egos depend on it. We label people based on how we feel when they do things we don't like or that society has conditioned us to believe is wrong. The English language is filled with words that we use to pass moral judgments on others – whore, slut, stupid, lazy, irresponsible – just to name a few. Those words, however, say nothing about the person on whom we are passing judgment. Just because we call someone a whore, doesn't make her one. It says more about how we think than anything else. Judging others makes us feel superior when nothing could be further from the truth. We are all one, part of the same Universe. When we judge others, we are also setting the standard by which we are judged. And most of us fall short.

Spiritual teacher and bestselling author Deepak Chopra wrote on his blog that judgments are from the ego-self that "wants to control life by imposing a simplistic black-or-white morality on everything... It may help to realize that everyone is doing the best they can with what they know at the time. Kindness and compassion from you will inspire them to do better and it will bring you closer to people's hearts as well."

When we judge others, we are creating a measure of that person's value and by doing so we are saying that we, too, have a certain value. I used to judge and criticize just about everything and everyone with whom I came into contact. Looking back, it didn't endear me to anyone. In fact, it kept me agitated and made me irascible. Took me out of the moment, the source of my power, my peace. And kept me separated from others as well.

Today, I shall judge nothing that occurs.

As someone who makes her living as an opinion writer, practicing non-judgment is especially challenging. But it's also especially rewarding to live that prayer, "Today, I shall judge nothing that occurs."

It means seeing the world and the people in it with different eyes. Recognizing that the same divine spirit that is the core of our being is the core of everyone's being. And at their core, the crack addict, the murderer, the liar and the cheater are no different than we are.

Nor is the president, the billionaire, the queen, or the most beloved celebrity. We all are operating at different levels of awareness. Some of us are at higher levels than others. The bottom line, though, is we are all the same. Not good, not bad. Not right and not wrong. We just are.

# LESSON #11

*When we judge others, we set the standard by which we want to be judged. Too often, it's a standard that we, ourselves, do not and cannot meet.*

## INNER WORK

### *THOU SHALT NOT JUDGE*

Take out a day to watch your thoughts and notice how often you judge other people.

Make note of how automatically you do it. Then take a day to watch your thoughts and make an effort to stop yourself from judging.

Now that you are aware of how automatically you do it, when you feel the judgmental thoughts coming, say to yourself, "I will judge nothing and no one."

This is easier when you make the effort to see others as souls or children of God instead of focusing on appearances.

Practice non-judgment using this technique daily.

# It's Not Me, It's You

~ When you take things personally, you feel offended, and your reaction is to defend your beliefs and create conflicts. You make something big out of something little, because you have the need to be right and make everybody else wrong. ~ Don Miguel Ruiz

It was the Wednesday before Thanksgiving and I was forcing myself out of bed, one open eye, and one leg out from under the covers at a time.

The alarm on the phone had gone off about a half hour earlier but I was still giving myself just five more minutes. Then my cell vibrated on the mattress next to me.

The voice on the other end forced me to sit up straight as I knew it had to be serious. My aunt is no more a morning person than I am.

For the sake of family, she said, it was time for me to forgive the grown man that had tried to have sex with my teenage daughter.

My aunt's daughter was hosting Thanksgiving dinner. I had informed her the day before that if her daughter's boyfriend, with whom she shared a home, was going to be there then I wouldn't.

I wasn't much in the mood to break bread with the man who had propositioned my 16-year-old daughter for sex. My aunt, though, wanted the family to be together.

"A judge, she said, "probably would've given him only six months' probation and it's already been longer than that." She went on to tell me that she had held her tongue before then to give me time to heal. She now felt that I had had enough time to get over what her daughter's boyfriend had tried to do to my daughter. "*A Course in Miracles* tells us," she said, "that we have to see him as guiltless. He does have some good qualities."

"I have forgiven him," I told her. "But what you don't seem to understand is that forgiveness is not about the other person it's about us. We forgive so that we're not holding on to toxic feelings and so we can move on. Just because I forgive him doesn't mean I have to have Thanksgiving dinner at his house."

She went on to tell me that I was "rationalizing" and "intellectualizing."

Not really. The reality is that forgiving someone and choosing whether or not to share their company are two separate decisions.

Forgiving does not mean condoning, nor does it mean forgetting. Forgiveness is to release us from the pain and anger - real and perceived - that we inflict upon ourselves and that others inflict upon us.

My aunt, though, wasn't trying to hear that. In the end, I let her know that though I appreciated the love behind her request I wouldn't be able to accommodate her wishes to join them for the holiday.

Her words, though, "rationalizing" and "intellectualizing" stayed with me the whole day as I wondered whether she was right. If I were as spiritually evolved as I thought, why wouldn't I just suck it up and join them? My aunt had told me that we had to be at peace. Before her call, I was at peace!

I bring up this story because it's a great example of how we let others make us question and judge ourselves by taking what they say and do personally. Even though I was OK with my decision to spend the holiday alone reading and writing, suddenly I was wondering whether I should attend the dinner just to prove that my aunt was wrong. That I was at a higher place. Of course, that was my ego talking. Suddenly I was obsessed with what others thought about me. That is a special kind of hell that the ego takes us to.

Not taking anything personally is the second agreement in Don Miguel Ruiz' *The Four Agreements*. "Nothing others do is because of you," he writes. "What others say and do is a projection of their own reality, their own dream. When you are immune to the opinions of others, you won't be the victim of needless suffering."

I knew this already. It's actually one of the most important lessons I believe I've learned on this journey, but how easy it was to forget!

That's not to say that I don't respect my aunt's opinion. I very much do. She is a very wise woman and I love her dearly. I knew that her intentions were good. Yet, that didn't stop my ego from going into full throttle and taking her words personally. Though she said, "I'm not judging," it certainly felt to me that she was doing exactly that.

I went to work the next day feeling as though a thousand ants were having a picnic on the contents of my stomach. Thoughts were running a marathon across my mind. I couldn't concentrate. Late in the afternoon, even though I had a deadline fast approaching and I was nowhere near finished, I left the office for an hour to try and find clarity.

I was struggling with the question of whether I was as enlightened as I believed. When my aunt was quoting *A Course in Miracles,* my ego heard her telling me I wasn't where I should be.

Dancing to the Rhythm of My Soul

The next morning while meditating, I found the clarity for which I'd been searching. My spiritual journey is *my* spiritual journey. I am exactly where I'm supposed to be. No one else can tell me where I should be. It's not a race or a competition. By staying home on Thanksgiving, I was doing what was comfortable for me. I wasn't trying to make a statement or do anything to anyone else.

My aunt had said that spiritually I could be where she wanted me to be "in the next second" if I had wanted to. But my journey is not about where she or anyone else wants me to be. Neither is yours. No one can walk outside of their own experience and into someone else's. We can't live in someone else's reality. We can only live in our own.

My aunt had said that we should be at peace. I realized that morning that she was the one who wasn't at peace. It wasn't an issue of my being right and her being wrong. Instead of accepting what was, she wanted me to get to a place where my actions would coincide with her desires. That would have made her feel better. It would not have made me feel better. And as much as I wanted to please her, I needed to please me more.

We can't live according to the expectations of others. When we do, we make ourselves miserable. The only person's opinion of you that matters is your own. At the same time, we must realize that our opinion of others is of no consequence to them, either!

By taking the words of my aunt personally, I put myself through an entire day of needless suffering. My day would have gone much more smoothly had I just taken what she said as her reality and not tried to defend myself.

We scoff at the phrase, "It's not you, it's me," because it's the break up line people use when they are copping out. Truer words, though, are rarely spoken! Think about the angst you have gone through because you took someone else's words or actions personally. Could you have spared yourself that turmoil by telling yourself, it's not me, it's him? Or her?

Carmen definitely could have saved herself a boat load of aggravation had she chosen not to take Chance's behavior personal. Chance had a habit of making plans and not following through. He was the king of no-call, no show. Whenever Chance was supposed to join us for tennis, dinner or some other event, I always assumed he wasn't going to show up and planned accordingly. Not Carmen.

She would get so angry she could spit fire. She would yell and scream at him and practically convulse whenever she confronted him about his behavior. She would stop taking his calls and at one point stopped speaking to him altogether.

Once, she invited him to a get-together at her house and he wouldn't commit. He said he might show up, but didn't know for sure. She demanded a yes or no. When she went into a tirade over his failure to give her a definitive answer, he told her that the reason he wouldn't commit was because he didn't want her to get mad if he didn't show up.

I asked Carmen why she let Chance get to her. She said that she just couldn't tolerate his inconsideration because that's not how friends behave.

"Sweetie, we all have issues," I told her. "Friends accept each other, flaws and all. You act as though Chance has singled you out for his behavior. This is just how he is. He doesn't wake up and say, 'Let me piss Carmen off today.' He does it to all of us. You're just the only one who takes it personal."

At first, she wasn't having it. She wanted - better yet her ego wanted - to make it about Chance being wrong and her being right. I explained that right and wrong had nothing to do with it. Chance was off doing his thing enjoying himself and she was sitting there about to have a coronary. The only person affected by her anger was her.

Chance wasn't going to change and she had to make a choice. Either she was going to be his friend, accepting those things about him that she

155

didn't like. Or she was going to end the friendship. Otherwise she was just going to continue to drive herself nuts.

Eventually, she saw the light and realized that it wasn't worth the effort that it took to be angry with Chance all the time. Carmen now just brushes her shoulders off when it comes to Chance's no-call, no shows. She has accepted that his behavior has nothing to do with her and everything to do with him. She actually can laugh at it all now.

What other people say and do is not a reflection of us. It is a reflection of them and where they are on their journey through this earthly experience. And where they are is where they are supposed to be. It's not for us to judge but to accept. And if it's an issue that we cannot tolerate, it's our choice whether to stay in the relationship or leave. After all, we picked them.

Unfortunately, Terrance has still not quite reached that place with his estranged wife. He takes just about everything that she does personally. You might think it's impossible to do otherwise, but I'm sure a lot of relationships would improve if we could get a little more perspective about why the people closest to us do what they do.

Terrance wants his wife to respect him as a father. He has always been there for their children physically, emotionally, and financially.

In many ways, he's been there far more than his wife. Yet, because she continues to hold on to grudges from Terrance's past indiscretions – infidelity being chief among them - she can't separate his performance as a husband from his performance as a father. So she undermines him. She tells the children about all of his indiscretions and makes it clear that they don't have to listen to or obey him.

Terrance says his wife has the right to her anger and he recognizes that he has issues. But he wants her to recognize his role as a father. He attributes her attitude to not having a father in her life. He says that her mother taught her that men were no good and she is teaching the same to their daughters.

"She should be able to see the difference between her father - who wasn't there for her - and me," he said angrily. "I've always taken care of my kids."

Terrance is particularly upset because he, too, grew up without a dad. Because of that, he works hard to be a better father to his children than his father was to him.

I tried to talk Terrance down from boil to simmer by explaining to him that his wife is operating at her level of awareness. What she's doing is all that she is capable of. If she knew better, she would do better. And none of it has anything to do with him.

"But," he kept insisting, "She should...."

"You keep telling me what she should do," Terrance," I said. "That's the problem. You're not recognizing that there's absolutely no correlation between what she does and what *you* think she *should* do."

What he thinks she should do is based on his knowledge and his level of awareness, not hers. He is expecting her to live up to something of which she is incapable – his expectations. And when she doesn't, he takes it personally.

Stacey, on the other hand, takes her children's actions – or lack of actions – as personally as she does her husband's. When, for instance, her children don't do their chores, she takes it as a sign that they don't love or appreciate her. When they don't meet her expectations, she sees it as a reflection on her. The reality is they are, like most teenagers, self-centered and forgetful. Like most children, they don't see doing their chores as an expression of love. How much better would Stacey feel if she saw her children's behavior for what it really is instead of as a personal affront?

She might feel like Amy, who has no problem tolerating her husband's grumpiness a few days a month because she knows it has nothing to do with her. She calls this time of month her husband's "period." Every thirty days or so, for no apparent reason, he snaps at her and gets agitated over the least little thing. In the beginning of their marriage, she would cry and wonder what she was doing wrong. Eventually, she figured out that it's just his nature to get that way. Now, when he acts out she doesn't respond in a way that feeds the negative energy, knowing that it will all be over in a few days. And she no longer wonders what she should be doing differently or what is wrong with her. In other words, she doesn't take it personally.

When we choose not to take things personally we choose to not be offended. We choose not to make what others do and say about us. We choose a far less emotionally turbulent and far more peaceful existence.

# LESSON #12

*What others do and say reflects who they are. It's not about us.*

## INNER WORK

### *DON'T TAKE IT PERSONAL*

Take note the next time you feel offended by someone else's words. Don't react and be defensive. Instead, count to 10. Then ask yourself why you feel the need to defend yourself. Is what he or she said true? If it is, then own it. If it's something you want to change, then do so. If not, so be it.

If it's not true, then why worry about it? Just because this person thinks it true doesn't make it so. Your thoughts about yourself are all that matters.

Do this exercise whenever something offends you. Eventually, you'll find that you get offended - and your feelings hurt – far less often. When you are not defending yourself or licking your wounds, you have more time to enjoy yourself.

# Let the Journey Begin

~ *There are only two mistakes one can make along the road to truth; not going all the way, and not starting.* ~ Buddha

The decision to make change in our lives can come suddenly or gradually. An unexpected event, a life altering experience or simply a desire to grow can prompt us to seek a different path.

Many people discover their divinity through a near death experience, a tragic illness or the diagnosis of a life changing disease.

Actor Michael J. Fox, who has for years had Parkinson's disease, describes his medical condition as a gift. "It's really opened me up to being a more kind of passionate, curious, risk-taking person," he said in an interview with CNN's Dr. Sanjay Gupta. "It's like being in the moment. It's just like there's no more important moment than right now."

# Dancing to the Rhythm of My Soul

When my mother lost her second leg to amputation nearly twenty years after losing the first, my initial response was anger over the unfairness of it all. Why her? I wondered.

"Why not me?" she answered. "I can take it."

My mother told me that the medical crises she endured were God's way of testing her. Of molding her. Of slowing her down and getting her to see what is important in life.

Sure she gets depressed, she told me. But then she thinks of her children and grandchildren and all the people who still depend on her for encouragement and she knows she still has a purpose. My mother realizes that she is not defined by her body. Even with one good limb, she still can serve others and that's why she's still here.

When we recognize our purpose and understand that the present moment is all that matters, we not only have tremendous peace, we have tremendous power.

Though many people experience a catastrophic illness or other negative life event such as divorce, losing a loved one, losing a job, or going to jail before they decide to take the journey of self-discovery, it doesn't have to be that way for you.

It doesn't have to take hitting rock bottom or becoming sick and tired of being sick and tired before we set foot on the path.

We can start our journey from anywhere. Our spiritual quest can begin in our living room, our bedroom, our workplace, or the shower. We only need the desire and the willingness to do the inner work.

"The spiritual path is our natural path, is the reason we are here in these bodies on this planet. And in order to walk a spiritual path, it is necessary to reprogram the mental perspectives of life that we learned growing up in a spiritually hostile, shame-based society," says spiritual teacher and therapist Robert Burney, author of *Codependence: The Dance of Wounded Souls.* "Perhaps the first, and certainly the most nurturing, thing we do when starting to walk a spiritual path is to start seeing life in a growth context - that is to start realizing that life events are lessons, opportunities for growth, not punishment because we screwed up or are unworthy. We are spiritual beings having a human experience not weak, shameful creatures who are here being punished or tested for worthiness. We are part of/an extension of an all-powerful, unconditionally loving god-force/goddess energy/great spirit, and we are here on earth going to boarding school not condemned to prison."

We are here to learn and to share what we've learned with others. We are not here to suffer or to prove our worthiness to make it into heaven or some other after-life paradise.

Paradise is here. We can live it every day by remembering who we truly are and by staying present. Presence brings us the gift of peace. As someone who daydreams often, I know what it is to constantly live in the future. The future always seems like a better place, doesn't it? The reality is that believing the future will bring us happiness by giving us the things we lack in the present is an illusion.

Whenever I find myself daydreaming now, I pull myself back to the present by being grateful for what I already have. It doesn't get any better than right now. That's because right now is all we've got!

I came onto the path after my cousin Benn told me that I still could have a spiritual life even though I no longer attended church. Organized religion had long since failed to provide me the spiritual nourishment I needed. I attended church out of habit and because it was a family obligation.

When I left my hometown, I no longer had that obligation. There were no family run churches in Virginia. Still, I sought out a church experience because it was what I was used to. I relished the opportunity to choose my own church instead of having it chosen for me. And I was hoping to find something different that would meet my needs.

I quickly realized that I wasn't going to find it in church.

Organized religion teaches me what to believe and insists that I ask no questions, even when those beliefs don't make sense. It teaches me that I came into this world an unworthy sinner and I have to earn mercy, grace and forgiveness or I will spend eternity burning in hell.

That's never made sense to me. A loving god would not punish his children this way. Since I couldn't wrap my mind around such beliefs or many other tenets of organized religion, I opted out.

Spirituality is not about beliefs. It's about truths that we learn to discern for ourselves. It's perfectly alright to ask questions, search for answers, and discard that which doesn't make sense.

I discovered this after my cousin prompted me to read Gary Zukav's *Seat of the Soul.* I haven't stopped reading, learning and growing since. Growth comes by putting into practice that which we learn.

Just as it takes years for a baby to become an adult, growth and change don't come overnight. But they do come if we commit to staying on the path.

The spiritual path is one we travel daily, not because we want to reach a destination but because we want to experience the journey. It's a lifelong journey, not a quick trip. There will be obstacles and crossroads along the way. There will be experiences that will be tougher than others, such as my surprising breast cancer diagnosis shortly after I finished writing this book. (I've added an extra chapter at the end if you want to know more.)

If you veer off the path, you can always get back on and press forward. There's no need to judge yourself or feel guilty.

The reward doesn't come at the end of the journey. It comes every step along the way as we experience happiness, peace of mind, inner peace, inner power and freedom. The freedom to be exactly who we were meant to be.

Enlightenment is a process. I am not where I would like to be, but I'm certainly not where I used to be.

When you are ready to begin your journey, the path will be there. It's up to you to take the first step.

# The Journey
# Never Ends

*Don't be afraid your life will end; be afraid that it will never begin. Grace Hansen*

When I began writing this book three years ago, I had two breasts and no expectations that would ever change. Today, thanks to cancer, I have one. As I began to pen this final chapter, a surprise, late addition that I had no idea I'd be writing, I was deciding whether or not to follow the mutilation of mastectomy with poisonous chemotherapy and cancer-causing radiation. Those are the treatments my doctors recommend. I've decided on a more natural, holistic approach to healing that will not include chemo or radiation.

Some of my loved ones would prefer that I do these traditional therapies because they believe these treatments are my best option for survival.

I have assured them that I am not on a suicide mission and that whatever treatment I choose; it will be an informed decision that I believe is in my best interest. It will not, though, be a decision made in fear.

Not that I'm immune to fear. Thoughts of death have invaded my mind several times since cancer forced me to face my mortality. I pull myself out of those dark moments by remembering who I truly am. I am a spiritual being having a human experience. Life is eternal. Though my body, which is temporary housing, will one day deteriorate and expire, the spirit that dwells within will live forever.

I don't know why cancer chose me. And I quickly gave up trying to figure out what I could've done to prevent it. I need to live in the present. I can't conquer cancer from a past that doesn't exist. Fear of a future that doesn't exist won't help me either.

The only place I have power is in the present.

So I go to the Word. I read the teachings of spiritual teachers. I meditate. I pray. I repeat mantras that speak my healing into existence.

I no longer watch news that I find utterly frustrating and depressing. I avoid violent TV shows and movies. I watch programs that educate me, lift my spirit, or make me laugh. I listen to music that inspires me, makes me smile and want to dance. (My new favorite song is *I Am Healed* by Jonathan Nelson.)

A close friend asked how I, someone she considers spiritually aware, physically active and healthy – someone who hasn't eaten meat in over a decade - could get cancer. Stuff happens, I told her. Then I reminded her that I wasn't always the woman she sees today.

I spent many years being miserable, angry and defensive. Many years so focused on what I didn't have that I couldn't be grateful for the many blessings I did have. I also complained often about my breasts and all the ways I found the mountains atop my chest annoying.

And I harbored a secret fear that I would be like my mother. That a life threatening medical condition would befall me at the same age that a stroke robbed my mother of her left side and her independence. Her medical crisis struck at 47. Mine at 48.

I don't know for sure whether any of those things contributed to my cancer diagnosis. They certainly are facts of my life I can't escape. I choose, however, not to dwell on or feel guilty about them.

My friend didn't like my response. She said it meant that even if we change for the better, the way we lived our lives in the past can still come back to haunt us.

That's life, I told her. Then I shared with her how grateful I am for enlightenment.

## Dancing to the Rhythm of My Soul

I decided early on that if the biopsy revealed cancer then it was something I had to go through to learn a lesson. A lesson I was meant to share with others.

I don't know what the lesson is. I do know that since the July 3, 2012 diagnosis, I have experienced the beauty of love like never before.

Love from family members who took turns flying to Florida to wait on me hand and foot after the mastectomy. Love from my significant other, David, who has been my sounding board and a shoulder upon which to rest my cares since the first suspicious mammogram. Love from friends who consistently let me know I'm in their thoughts and prayers.

I've even experienced love from strangers, such as the staff at the hospital where I lost my left breast and from women I've never met who have conquered cancer like me. I say conquered because I believe that I am already healed. That's why I wrote on the back cover of this book that I *am* a cancer conqueror. Regardless of which treatment I choose, I believe it will work, so I have already claimed it.

I practice gratitude daily, expressing my thanks when I awake for each day I get to see. I give praise for my healing and the profound love that continues to rain down on me. For the spiritual growth and development that allows me to face cancer without self-pity. For the strength I've discovered along the way.

I told my girlfriend that cancer will show you who you really are. It's certainly doing that for me. When I went into the hospital it was supposed to be for a lumpectomy followed by radiation. When I awoke from surgery, however, my doctor informed me that the cancer was invasive and she advised me to have a mastectomy.

I was groggy, still coming out from under anesthesia and on morphine for pain. The worried look on my doctor's face and the urgency in her voice made me feel as though this was the only choice to save my life. I agreed and 24 hours later she performed the surgery.

I'd had no time to research mastectomies or what they do to the body. I've learned that I may never again have feeling under my arm or in the area where my breast used to be. My surgeon says my brain will eventually shut off the signal that tells me I have no feeling in that area so I won't notice it as much. I can't wait.

I will forever have to remind myself not to hang my purse from my left shoulder because doing so could cause lymphedema, incurable swelling in my arm as a result of the excision of the 16 lymph nodes in my armpit, only two of which had evidence of cancer.

But regrets are useless. Though I'd advise other women facing this choice to take their time and first do the research - a few days will not matter - I choose not to long for my missing breast and wish I'd made a different choice. I simply have decided never to make another decision based on fear – mine or anyone else's.

That's not who I am.

"For God hath not given us the spirit of fear," says II Timothy 1:7, "but of power, and of love, and of a sound mind."

If I remove fear from the equation, I have the power of love and free will and the intellect of my sound mind to make the best choices for myself. Choices made in the absence of fear bring me peace of mind.

Though I'd consented to chemo and radiation immediately after the surgery, I changed my mind weeks later. I realized that a scared person made that decision.

A woman confident in her faith and the body's ability to heal itself has made the decision to worship my temple. I am nourishing my body, ridding it of environmental toxins and rebuilding my immune system with an organic, raw food diet. And I am searching for and releasing any unconscious negative energy that lurks within. Healing is a mental and spiritual journey as much as it is a physical one.

I've concluded that cancer has come into my life to push me to the next level on my path. I don't know where I'm headed, but I am excited about what's next.

I will undoubtedly share this chapter of my life in future columns, possibly future books and on my blog, *Consciously Speaking,* which you can find on my website at www.rhondaswan.com. I hope you will check it out from time to time and wish me well on my healing journey.

We are all healing and I wish each and every one of you love, peace and joy on your journey. I wish for you the best life that you can create.

# ABOUT THE AUTHOR

Rhonda Swan is an award winning journalist and poet who works as an opinion writer for *The Palm Beach Post* in Florida. Her columns have appeared in newspapers across the United States, Canada and abroad.

She is sought after as a speaker, panelist and moderator by numerous organizations.

Rhonda worked 12 years as a reporter covering a variety of beats before becoming an editor. She has worked as an editor at the Daily Press in Virginia, the News-Journal in Delaware and at The Palm Beach Post.

She has taught journalism at the University of Massachusetts and at Springfield College. She is the former host of the weekly radio talk show *The Spoken Word*, a platform she used to educate, enlighten and encourage the listening community.

She is the author of a novel, *Busted: Never Underestimate a Sista's Revenge*, and a volume of poetry titled, *Speaking My Mind in Poetic Verse*.

*Dancing to the Rhythm of My Soul* is her first full-length non-fiction work.

Rhonda is the mother of three adult children and has one grandchild.

## PERMISSIONS

Grateful acknowledgment is made to the following for permission to reprint copyrighted material:

Dancing to the Rhythm of My Soul

Reprinted from various sources with by permission of Mary McWilliams.